Contemporary Museums

*To my father, Nicola,
and my mother, Paola*

Antonello Marotta

Contemporary Museums

Cover
Zaha Hadid Architects
Landesgardenschau
Meyer, Scherer & Rockcastle
Mill City Museum
Zaha Hadid Architects
*Maxxi National Centre
of Contemporary Arts*
Tadao Ando Architect
& Associates
Modern Art Museum
Daniel Libeskind
Jewish Museum Berlin
Shigeru Ban Architects
Bianimale Nomadic Museum
UN Studio
*New Mercedes Benz
Museum*

Back cover
Paulo David
*Arts Centre – Casa Das
Mudas*

Editor
Luca Molinari

Design
Marcello Francone

Editorial Coordination
Giulia Valcamonica

Editing
Elena Bajetta, Marta Cattaneo

Layout
Paola and Flavio Ranzini

Translations
Robert Burns for Language
Consulting Congressi, Milan

Iconographical Research
Antonello Marotta
Alessandra Mion

Entries by
Antonello Marotta

First published in Italy in 2010
by Skira Editore S.p.A.
Palazzo Casati Stampa
via Torino 61
20123 Milano
Italy
www.skira.net

© 2010 Skira editore, Milan
© Jean Nouvel,
UN Studio / Van Berkel & Bos
by SIAE 2010

Printed and bound in Italy.
First edition

ISBN: 978-88-572-0258-7

Distributed in North America
by Rizzoli International
Publications, Inc.,
300 Park Avenue South,
New York, NY 10010, USA.
Distributed elsewhere
in the world by Thames
and Hudson Ltd.,
181A High Holborn, London
WC1V 7QX, United Kingdom.

Acknowledgements
My heartfelt thanks to
Christine Tilley for having
handled, over the past five
years, contacts with the
various architecture studios
around the world and for her
ready helpfulness and
friendship; to Luana Gugliotta
for her unflagging support
throughout this project; to my
friends and teachers, Mario
Dell'Acqua, Manlio Brusatin,
Sebastiano Bagnara and
Antonino Saggio, who have
provided me with a sounding
board and invaluable
nourishment; to Giulia
Valcamonica, Elena Bajetta
and Marta Cattaneo for their
care in editing, Robert Burns
for translations, Flavio and
Paola Ranzini for their work on
the layout, and Marcello
Francone for graphic design.
My grateful thoughts also go
to Carlo Manzo and
Massimiliano Rendina for the
time and effort they dedicated
to me during the three deeply
reflective years of my doctoral
work. Lastly, I owe many
thanks to Luca Molinari for the
extraordinary opportunity
I have had to delve into these
themes.

Contents

Museum and Public Space: from library to interwoven space

The place dedicated to memory, to perpetuating the continuity of human action, originated at the beginning as an inscription of traces: the first inscriptions were the signs engraved in rock and the apotropaic symbols in the caves; later, when societies established that knowledge could be classified, the inscriptions took the form of written graphemes. Writing represented the space of memory, when time was formalised for the first time in a message that could be transcribed for future memory.

Back in the 3rd and 2nd millennia BCE, temples, palaces and libraries in the Mesopotamian culture were the first proto-museums, as Virgilio Vercelloni tells us in *Cronologia del museo*. They were places where knowledge began to be conserved and communicated. The origin of the word 'museum' is attributed to the revolution sparked by Ptolemy II Philadelphus, who erected a *mouseion*, dedicated to the muses, in Alexandria, Egypt in the 3rd century BCE. It included a huge library and collection of art and objects produced by scientists and engineers.[1] Over the centuries, these places took on different characteristics, orientations and functions.

In the Renaissance, with its need to bring back to life a golden past, the theme of memory once again became something that was alive and pulsating. The museum became a place for study, thanks to the great collections of the Medici, Gonzaga and Sforza families. Here, patrons or aristocrats selected, collected, and assembled often heterogeneous arrays of relics and knowledge to which access was granted only to select groups of intellectuals and scholars. Over time, these accumulations would end up in the collections of official museums, becoming the heritage of all.

The 16th century witnessed an interpretation of the museum as a *theatre*, embracing two parallel visions: the *theatre of memory* and the *theatre of nature*. Giulio Camillo's *Teatro della memoria*, conceived in the 16th century as a model for an ideal mnemonic construct, was intended to collect and summarise all human knowledge. Camillo had thought up this place as a universal device. It was ideated, according to certain critics, along the lines of the seven Vitruvian orders, and sought to categorise all knowledge into a grid of 49 boxes, each one assigned to a divinity in keeping with the then current dictates of mnemotechny. It was the stream into which flowed cabalistic conceptions linked to astrology and numerology. In this phase, there was a strong resurgence of the Platonic ideals and knowledge entered a complex sphere, capable of creating a universal museum. Manlio Brusatin points out that Camillo's *Teatro* must have been an interwoven space: a mix of laboratory and library.[2]

These ideal devices had found an extraordinary alliance in the military engineers who not only built defensive devices but also studied mechanisms for increasing knowledge. In 1588 Agostino Ramelli had published in Paris *The Diverse and Artifactitious Machines of Captain Agostino Ramelli*, including his outstanding design (no. 188) for a 'book wheel,' a sort of vertically revolving bookstand which allowed scholars to shift from one book to another with the simple action of a foot pedal. With its epicyclic gearing, this mnemonic museum-machine embodied the Renaissance desire for absolute knowledge.[3]

Hence the museum, as a remembrance or unveiling, turns to the constructive mechanisms of language. Frances Yates, in her book *The Art of Memory*, retracing the studies of the 13th-century Catalan philosopher and mystic Raimondo Lullo as well as those of Giulio Camillo and Giordano Bruno (16th century), described these extraordinary machines of memory, tools capable of generating thought, in which language and reminiscence were translated into increasingly diversified and specialised milieux. To strengthen the mind was the dream of the intellectual at the service of power.[4]

In the mid-16th century, the erudite scholar from Bologna Ulisse Aldrovandi began accumulating botanical and zoological specimens, a sort of *Teatro della natura*. The collection was an attempt to classify species from the organic and inorganic world with a strictly scientific intent. At the same time, the scholar sought to demonstrate the relation between the creation of man and the creation of nature. When he died, in 1605, the Museo Aldrovandiano was instituted at the University of Bologna to house the extensive collections produced through a life of research. This need to systematise knowledge was sparked by a number of different transformations. These included both the discovery of the New World and the new plant species there that had thrown all of medieval taxonomy into disarray, and the scientific innovations initially ushered in by Copernicus regarding the heliocentric nature of the solar system. With respect to the Ptolemaic system, which placed the earth at the centre of the universe, the Copernican revolution forced man, who had lost his central position, to analyze and comprehend the rules governing the functioning of the world.

In parallel, the *Wunderkammern* [cabinets of curiosities] appeared in Europe in the 16th century, set up as a means for assembling a multivarious array of objects in an atmosphere of pre-scientific wonderment.[5] The method of organising the collections was based on *naturalia*, objects from the kingdom of nature, and *mirabilia*, organic or inorganic materials testifying to human engineering, with the illusory goal of overcoming the barrier between natural and human. It was a way of seeking an encyclopaedic culture, whose etymology, like the wheel or heavenly orbs, evoked the cyclical nature of knowledge. As Vercelloni wrote: 'to the private and subjective *Wunderkammer*, the 16th century counterposed the epistemological leap of the objective, ordered and systematic *theatre of the world*.'[6] The difference between the Italian *teatro* and the German *Kammer* lay in their intent: the former was scientific in nature, the latter sought to amaze the visitor with curious and rare objects. Lacking any systematic order, such as that in the Italian scientific museum of Aldrovandi, the real knowledge contained in the *Kammern* remained veiled. The intention of the nobleman who had spent huge sums of money on his collection was to generate amazement and awe in the visitor. They were rooms similar to laboratories in which all sorts of novelties, curiosities and early machines were accumulated. These cabinets also evinced the strong relationship between creativity and instruments, between nature and artifice, shifting the boundary line toward an unknown space that was necessarily metaphorical and symbolic, a filter between life and death, a place of interchange between the realities that surround and confound us.

These places heralded the idea of a ludic museum, of the unexpected, and opened the way, in time, to a vision of museum design as a workshop or laboratory, as many new structures are conceived today. The *Wunderkammern* continued into the 18th century, introducing the first automatons with the dawning of the industrial revolution.

In the 18th century, in a climate of enlightenment, Diderot and D'Alembert supervised the creation of the *Encyclopédie*. It would render knowledge of physics scientific, cataloguing and systematising the knowledge of the time and effectively decreeing the end of the eclectic and heterogeneous German museums. The archaeological discoveries of Pompeii and Herculaneum had favoured a rebirth of the classical style and, over time, dictated the need to design complex and diversified showcases in the city to receive and display the documents of the past. In the same period, Johann Joachim Winckelmann, inspired by the archaeological findings and with a predilection for Greek culture, published the *History of Ancient Art* (1764).

In 1789, the French Revolution not only altered humanity's social vision but also generated the need to open museums to a broad audience. Part of the pedagogical thinking of the Jacobins was that Beauty, accessible to all visitors, was a grounding principle for the idea of Virtue. Bringing back to life Greek *kalokagathia*, the ideal of the body and the city based on equilibrium, justice and proportion, meant offering, via the institution of the museum, a model for moral virtue that would lead to the forging of a new society.

On 18 November 1793, the galleries of the Louvre were opened to the general public, changing the status of the museum from a birthright for the few to a civil right for all. The main characteristic of the new institution was that it was to transmit a feeling of national belonging. The museum, as we now conventionally think of it, arose from the desire to make knowledge a collective heritage.

The 19th century witnessed the construction of the first museums in the world's major capitals of the time.

The neoclassical museum was conceived, *ante litteram*, as a sort of hypertext. In a classicist and eclectic vision, it was translated into a complex model that incorporated the grammatical memories of the past into its shell.

There was a return of Classical tympana, Ionic columns, suggestive of a temple, and Roman pilaster strips, and once again the spaces of vaulted ceilings or domes inspired by 16th-century architecture. In this interpretation, whereby architecture replicated its DNA, the museum not only took in works, as a display and conservation of the past, but more importantly, it framed, in its spacious box, all other preceding memories. The museum and the city were considered inseparable entities.

In the years 1815–30, Leo von Klenze created the *Glyptothek* in Munich. It was conceived as a Classical temple that would house not only the marble statues, but also the mental structures of Classical culture. Between 1823-28, Karl Friedrich Schinkel built the Altes Museum in Berlin, on an urban island in the Spree river, distinguished by a portico and continual rooms. It was an expression of the cultural, artistic, social, and certainly also the political stature of the city. In Vienna, Gottfried Semper completed the Kunsthistorisches Museum in 1891 as a palace of culture, designed on the model of the Renaissance linear succession of spaces. These buildings exhibited an interior complexity, both in the spaces dedicated to contemplation and in those that were more strictly urban complements. The museum-palace witnessed the apex of splendour in this phase in which culture and power merged to communicate an image of memory, a mirror of a new social sense or of aspirations to an ideal.[7]

As a consequence, the very substance and constitution of the 19th-century museum registers time past with a renewed enthusiasm for styles as a form of archaeological memory. In this phase it achieved a perfect harmony between the works kept there, which were often purloined and transported from one continent to another, and its own physical makeup, in being conceived as an urban, political and social catalyst. Still today when we enter a 19th-century institution we feel a sense of awe, of reverence, and, if you will, of diversity between the subject and the representational space.

What happened in the first decades of the 20th century, at this central moment for understanding everything that would happen from then on?

With the 20th century and its wars and expunging bombardments, the city became a burnt library, a devoured location, an erased physical entity.

We must not forget myth: always a locus of mixed signifiers, always new, characterized by an extraordinary capacity to take on new meanings with the changing times and the changing conscience.

In Greek myth, as Károly Kerényi tells us, there were two rivers, located close to one another, the spring of *Mnemosyne*, temple of memory, and the house of *Lethe*, the space of oblivion.[8] These were two rivers that worked against each other to demonstrate that existence is always caught between these two instances, like two sides of the same coin. Memory and Oblivion have always been the two coordinate points which, together with *Kronos* (chronological time) and *Kairos* (psychological time), map out the geography of the individual. The former is sequential and quantitative time, the latter mental and indeterminate, like something caught somewhere in the middle. Epistemologists have explained that the structure of the mind has to remember to defend itself against experience and has to forget suffering in order to keep the system in equilibrium. Speaking of the museum today means facing the mythical time of memory and oblivion.

The rivers that contain the magic of memory and oblivion do not merely represent an archetypical dimension, but are unquestionably a metaphor for an idea of movement, dynamism, liquefaction of hierarchical structures.

In the 20th century, as a consequence, memory entered a conflictual space: memory is no longer the container, the scenery amidst which Raphael and later Palladio, in the eternal city of Rome, could extract and recover from the ruins the golden rules of the classical era, the geometrical and mathematical principles, ideally intact in their proportions.

On the other hand, the rubble from the destruction of the wars wiped away the hopes for a golden world, and made room for the Arabian phoenix, Klee's angel: a place of dissolution that would be a new starting point.

The Futurists were the ones to anticipate the change: taking speed and mobility to be the prime principles of the new era, marked by the need for resumption, for innovation to overcome a static conception of reality, they saw museums as an institution that was doomed to perish. Airplanes and trains were the new machines that gave humankind a new perspective on the city and, as a consequence, a new urban and social memory. Futurism denied the concept of a space designed for contemplation.

On 20 February 1909, Filippo Tommaso Marinetti published the article *Le Futurisme*, containing the *Futurist Manifesto*, in *Le Figaro*. In it he called for the burning of libraries and the demolition of museums. This dramatic idea, focussing on the need to annihilate time, prophetically prefigured the upheavals that would be caused by the war. The avant-garde movements, in their need to re-establish a violated order, stood in opposition to memory, they did not accept its conciliatory dimension. What prevailed was a need to zero things out, wipe the slate clean. But even more than Futurism, it was Dadaism that challenged the very idea of art.

Marcel Duchamp, modifying the semantic nature of objects, under-mined the very idea of memory. His transformed objects, the urinal that becomes a fountain, paradoxically restores meaning to the museum space, which now has to adapt to a new order in the relation between human perception and exhibition space.[9] The fountain, as a decontextualized work, would not make sense outside of the space conventionally meant for its viewing, and over time Dadaist works generated the need to conceive a new museum philosophy. The work no longer exists autonomously, but requires curious, astonished and enquiring onlookers. In the end, this trend makes the observer into an active participant who is capable of expressing judgements. Critics interpreted in the Dadaist movement the true breakup of the traditional idea of art and, as a consequence, of the need to build temples to future memory. If art changes, if the object transmutes into a déjà vu, into a *readymade*, this eliminates the need to preserve a modified or inexistent memory.

In the irreverent and revolutionary intentions of the Dada movement, which originated and developed at the start of the First World War (Zürich, 1916), poet and ideologue of the movement, Tristan Tzara introduced the first devices depending on chance, in a critical phase in history when repressive forces were suppressing conscience and constraining singular and collective individualities. In his poem *Pour faire un poème dadaïste* he wrote:

Take a newspaper.
Take a pair of scissors.
Choose an article as long as you are planning to make your poem.
Cut out the article.
Then cut out each of the words that make up this article and put them in a bag.
Shake it gently.

Then take out all the scraps one after the other.
Copy conscientiously in the order in which they left the bag.
The poem will be like you.
And here you are a writer, infinitely original and endowed with a sensibility that is charming though beyond the understanding of the vulgar.[10]

The poem invites people to undertake a deconstructed and random system of poetry writing that includes this ability to slice into, cut up and section reality. However, we know that, apart from a few experiments undertaken by Hans Jean Arp on fortuitous composition, the Dada movement never accomplished a concrete realization of its philosophy constructed around chance.

Tzara's poem expresses the artistic conception and act as a combinatory dynamic but, upon careful reading, the writing principle is quite precise and orderly.[11]

The movement created a new correlation between the visual and textual means of producing a work, bringing about a profound line of demarcation in the philosophy of the time. The avant-garde culture of the 20th century, while driven by political motives to deny the role of the museum, would create the future conception of the museum as a relational space and no longer as one suited to the interpretation of individual works.

As a consequence, we enter into a view that poses serious questions, not only regarding the role of the museum, but more deeply regarding its very semantic and signifying nature.

The museum cannot be conceived as a mere essential space. The walls of the Louvre were conceived so that they could receive the main actor, the painting, which in its nature translated itself into a frame that demarcated the space of the support: a sort of window that threw open the mind of the observer to the artist's imaginative representation.

The space of contemporary art, transforming the same expressive materials into something other than a painting or a sculpture, introduced new dynamics that no longer regarded neutral and aseptic backgrounds.

This new dimension of space and time was visualized via the invocation of the form of the upward spiral as an integral part of a dream of a desire for overcoming. The most intense and profound image was summoned in 1917 by Franz Kafka in his short story *The Great Wall of China*. The writer brought together in this piece two figures that had always remained disjoint in mythological imagination: the great wall, conceived as a sort of semi-circle, and the Tower of Babel. In his expressive vision he causes them to converge, colliding and becoming superimposed, into the mass of a contemporary and strongly idealized construction. The tower failed due to weaknesses in its foundations. Kafka transposed this limitation as the crisis of the foundations of modern humanity. In this conceptual process we discern his ability to disassemble and give new life to the Myth, an anti-Classical and anti-idolatrous myth, that opens the way to the indefinite.

Just two years later, in a climate generated by the Russian Revolution, Vladimir Tatlin, with his Monument to the Third International (1919), created an antecedent in the history of the 20th century: a tilting, tormented spiral, which introduced the demise of material structures in favour of strongly symbolic ideas.

At the close of the 1920s, these principles made inroads through plans on paper, determining a new dimension for memory, in parallel with the most innovative artistic quests.

It was Le Corbusier, a complex and tormented architect, who anticipated in 1929, with the World Museum in Geneva, an unbuilt work, the theme of the linear spiral. Designed reminiscent of the archaeological past of an Egyptian or Mayan pyramid, it proposed a new spatial and compositional conception. In 1929, and parallel to this, the New York Museum of Modern Art was founded, later erected in its current site on the island of Manhattan in 1939, reflecting an idea of progress and modernity to which American society aspired.

With his plans for a Museum of Unlimited Growth, in 1939 Le Corbusier developed the idea of an evolutionary spiral. It was structured upon a square and harked back to Renaissance labyrinths. The entrance, located in the central space, liberated the expositional machine, which could evolve infinitely along the always open axis of the myth. It was the modern utopia, capable of growing within a constantly progressive dynamic.[12]

In this work, the architect inquires into the need to build a model that can be developed and expanded over time and that offers a wide array of possible configurations.

Le Corbusier's museographic projects bear witness to a radical transformation in the way of conceiving the representation of space and time.

The sequential and linear timeframe of the exhibition, trailing through different rooms, belonged to the conception of the museum existing from the Renaissance to the 19th century. With the revolution introduced by Einstein starting in 1905 and formalized in 1915 with his Theory of Relativity, contemporaneous with the birth of Expressionism, a new interpretation of time, and consequently space, was fostered.

Le Corbusier broke up an enduring institutional image of the museum and introduced the theme of personalization of space.

Furthermore, the spiral is the geometrical figure that best upholds the classical rule of the golden section: think of the structure of the Nautilus.

In 1959, Frank Lloyd Wright completed the Solomon Guggenheim Museum in New York, establishing a new conceptual view of the museum and the space it inscribes, based on the principle of a rising spiral. This marked an aspiration to verticality and growth that would go beyond the Biblical Tower of Babel.

The American architect broke with all conventional geometry and created a rather compact building within the New York urban space, but one that explodes as soon as one enters.

What has changed in this structure?

One thing certainly is the exhibition path that starts from above after an elevator ride to the top of the spiral ramp, along which the works are displayed. Wright had theorized another way of thinking of the museum, in which the spatial scenography created hidden relations between the works on display and the architecture that contains them. The observer's perception of the works changes. The work is no longer inserted into the categorical space of the 19th-century museum nor in the neutral space of the modernist white cube, but in a complex and articulate space characterized by zones of emptiness.

Wright generated a different mythology of the museum space, which naturally had its detractors, who claimed that the works were difficult to see because of the shadows cast by the ramp. The architect had shifted the interpretive axis: the space of the museum exists beyond the exhibited works, generating an internal contradiction between content and container which has now become the rule. With the Guggenheim, memory lives in the act of passing through substances, materials and thoughts.

This idea had been preannounced by Marcel Duchamp with his series of *Boîte-en-valise* [Box in a Valise], in which he had re-elaborated in a miniature form his works and accommodated them in a valise (1935–41), which could be packed up and taken from one venue to another. The French artist gave form to an idea of a museum as a passing, transitory thing. For Duchamp, memory is no longer static, but necessarily demands a contemporary sense of movement. The artist anticipated the transformation, opening an interpretive path for a nomadic space, at a time when the Modern Movement was crafting the museum as an absolute, metaphysical, pure space.

This brings us to a season in which museums often found themselves addressing the problem of making the message into a metaphor. The architecture is no longer neutral and the museum has to communicate, via its very fibres, the meanings for which it has originated and grown.

The Duchampian idea of the museum in movement took shape in the second half of the 20th century. In the 1960s, a number of trends arose toward developing architecture as a kinetic, dynamic machine. The structure became a mobile frame allowing flexibility of use. If Le Corbusier had thought of the museum as an organism that could expand along the dynamic and geometrical directrices of a spiral and Wright had given material form to a descending space as the physical realm of passage, with the quest of Archigram, the movements of society and political transformations are translated into the very processes of the architectural machine.

In 1961, Cedric Price anticipated this theory with his Fun Palace, a building featuring flexible space. But, like the plans of Sant'Elia developed some decades prior, Price's designs for the building remained on paper. It was Renzo Piano and Richard Rogers who gave material form to the idea of a dynamic and flexible architecture in the Pompidou Centre, built in 1971–77. The philosopher Jean Baudrillard and the architect Jean Nouvel discussed this machine and its capability of giving visual form to virtual space and the void in *The Singular Objects of Architecture*. The Beaubourg remains a potential project, the visualization of a mechanistic utopia. In the final analysis, the escalators and flexible spaces did not respond to the internal needs of a museum, but opened up the space to an interpretation of architecture detached from its contents. With the Beaubourg, the container registers the contradictions of the contemporary era and becomes an expressive and abstract structure, in many ways divorced from its artistic content.

Referring to the Parisian museum, Françoise Choay writes that 'The primary function assigned to the architecture of the Pompidou Centre is one of publicity. What it must do, first and foremost, is to attract the attention of potential visitors either there on the spot or via its image communicated through the media. Its primary characteristic is thus its iconic pregnancy, or more precisely its *imageabilité*, i.e., its ability to be reproduced in a form that has impact, through a two-dimensional copy. In other words, it is a genre that links back to the architecture-signal that characterizes post-urban agglomerations. In the context of the museum, this concept expresses the primacy of the container over its contents, given that it is precisely the packaging, that which the industry calls the "conditioning," that determines the influx of visitors.[13]

Having come down through the centuries, the theme of the museum, the house of the muses, representing the dwelling place of memory in ancient times, returns in these years with a pressing need for redefinition.

Museums transformed from the metaphysical containers of the modern era into archaeological envelopes in the late 1970s and 1980s, when interest was rekindled in the stratifications of the past.

Along these lines, Aldo Rossi created his *Teatro del Mondo* for the 1979 Architecture Biennial in Venice. It was a timeless museum, an internal and external scenery machine. The image that best characterizes it is its transportation on a barge, impalpable, under an embittered sky with muted colours, between the lightness of the water and the massive weight of its structure, between the ephemeral material image and its figurative iconicity enduring the stretch of history, juxtaposed with the buildings on Punta della Dogana.

In 1980, Daniel Libeskind dedicated himself to Rossi's *Teatro del Mondo* and Camillo's *Teatro della Memoria* in an article *Deus ex Machina / Machina ex Deo* published in *Oppositions*. He compared the two scenery systems and highlighted the fact that Rossi's interpretation of the theatre was a scenic apparatus that revealed a parallel reality and reconstructed the same memory.

The *Teatro del Mondo* invoked a space suspended between the water and the sky and reminded us that the poetry of ancient times could only live again within a matter that re-evoked the past.

In 1987, with his project for the Deutsches Historisches Museum in Berlin, Aldo Rossi offered new food for thought to museographic theorists. The museum testified to a way of sensing the city as a whole, as a unitary work of art, as the synthesis of a variety of experiences. The suggestions of medieval cities, the minimal units of the cabins on the Island of Elba and the Renaissance rotunda that played the role of interconnecting the various elements of the building are returned to us in an articulated whole. In the philosophy of Aldo Rossi, the project was adapted to a dual reference system, two arteries that indicated the location, the Paul Löbe Straße and the Spree River as territorial and urban markers. It is a new idea of the museum as the reminiscence on all of past history, a mysterious recollection suspended halfway between the earth and the sea.[14]

If the museum as a 19th-century institution was a hierarchical space that inspired awe and conveyed the ordering nature of power, in the 1990s it became a space that adapted itself to the varying needs and aspirations of the visitor. And that is not all. In this new conception of the container, architecture itself was translated, following upon the revolution introduced by Wright's

New York Guggenheim and after Libeskind's Jewish Museum and Gehry's Bilbao Guggenheim, into a work of art and the non-traversable scenic space became the new actor, more important than the works on display. This view tends to consider the museum as an experience, not solely didactic, but one relating to inner growth. The perception shifted from a monofocal conception, i.e., one concentrating on the work, often exalted by the neutralization of the support, to a stereophonic one, which sees the museum experience as a *summa* of stimuli: work and space, memory and relations, past and future. The interweave has replaced the categorical view of the positivist institutions.

Exchanging the support and the frame for new artistic expressions—from Dadaism, passing toward the end of the 1960s by way of Conceptual Art, Body Art, Happenings and Land Art—art drove architectural culture to create spaces suitable for complementing the new visions of the world.

The new expressions thus created the need to abandon the view of the museum as a framing space and conceive of it as a relational space.

In this change of perspective, we went from the modernist idea in which the work of art was the window through which we could read the outer world, to the contemporary, satellite idea of our times, marked by interferences, multiple registers, in which void space is more important than occupied space, in which relations are more determinant than the content of the single work, in which the dynamics of movement supplant the static and aprioristic categories of the past.

In 1989, with the victory of his Jewish Museum, Daniel Libeskind transformed the vision of the contemporary museum before Gehry reshaped the life in a small provincial town into a destination point for international tourism with the Bilbao Guggenheim (1991–97).

Libeskind addressed a still tormented history and in Berlin in 1998, against everyone's wishes (suffice it to think of the strong opposition within the building commission, from investors and on the part of many German citizens), realized a new organism that stands counter to the urban rule and transforms the urban layout into a map of trajectories, lines that connect places where intellectuals, poets, and artists of Jewish cultural extraction once lived. He then connected these lines into an informal design that transformed the place into an interweave of universal memory. The void that runs through the museum evokes the gaping wound of obliterated names and represents a unique and unrepeatable experience for visitors. It recounted the contemporary age. It actually did not need to have exhibits. No work could better describe the silence narrated by its anguished text.

After September 11, 2001, the Berlin museum is no longer the same. Two events have transformed it. New security measures oblige museum guides to have visitors enter via the nearby Kollegienhaus, the museum of the town history, whereas this descent had previously been a conquest by the visitor, who could, lacking a desire for discovery, go away, thinking that in the end the museum was just a closed, massive, symbolic work. But even worse, it has lost its peculiar power. It has been filled with descriptive exhibits, remembrances that would certainly be important in another place, but not in this one, not in this symbol of tragic memory, which as such should have been left empty in its own evocative silence.

Here we seem to enter a paradox. Can a museum contain nothing? In the case of the Jewish Museum in Berlin, I think the answer is yes. Like no other place of memory, the museum interpreted the space of collective relations in an autonomous and isolated place. It was able to put the observer into a state of doubt, into an experience of silence. An untranslatable message was communicated: there was nothing to understand. And it was so intense that the subject of the museum was its deafening void. It communicated, with the bareness of its walls, in the weak light of its narrow slits, the deprivation of existence, the impossibility of rendering rational the irrational, absurd, incomprehensible account of the extermination of an entire people.

With Gehry's museum in Bilbao and Libeskind's in Berlin, different in nature and function, architecture translated into an artistic representation. In many ways the content became less important and even absurdly irrelevant.

Gehry rendered his expressive machine spectacular. Like a futurist work, the Guggenheim hangs on the various directrices of the city. It translates into an urban sculpture, a landscape icon in the public space.

It is not possible to trace a line of demarcation in the history of architecture, a clear boundary where things happen or are cut off. The museum experience—which this volume sets out to trace along a path extending over the past twenty years—demonstrates differentiation of orientations and purposes. Nevertheless, what prevails, on different levels, is the idea that the museum has to communicate a complex set of meanings through its material manifestation and the way in which it relates to its context, in the information that it manages to transmit.

Along the line of transition from the 19th-century museum-showcase, to the modern museum-frame, to the museum-citation of the 1980s, to the museum-symbol of the 1990s, we come to the latest category: the museum-excavation.

In 1998, Steven Holl created the Kiasma Museum in Helsinki, wherein a new museum concept was formalized based on an interweave of spaces.

Holl tells us about it in his text *Parallax*. Parallax, first and foremost, is a phenomenon related to perception, the change in the perception of a surface with changes in vantage point.[15] We enter that which Pavel Florenskij has defined an overturned perspective, where we look at things from another point of view. In 1917, Viktor Borisovič Šklovskij wrote an important essay titled *Art as Device* [also translated *Art as Technique*]. Exposed to futurist expression, the Russian critic invited us to see what lies before our eyes, inured by habit, in a new light, with the aim of breaking with perceptive automatisms and making reality surprising. It is a process of 'defamiliarization' hinging on our capacity to give new meaning to conventional signifiers.

Hence, entering the world of parallax means thinking that even the museum itself may exist in a new light or according to a new interpretation.

While modern architects drew their inspiration from travels to ancient monuments, it is now their very creations of modernity that are generating a new contemporary archaeology. Holl was deeply influenced by two fundamental trips to the same place but at different times. In 1976 and 1999, he visited Le Corbusier's La Tourette. The Swiss architect had transposed, following a 1907 trip to Italy, the massiveness of the Certosa of Ema into the new project. For Holl, the most mystery-laden part of the whole thing was the empty space of the crypt at the convent. He did not fully grasp it until his second visit. He understood the power of that space. It is certainly the excavation that most strongly fascinated him in this critical review of the work of Le Corbusier, not the formal or figural aspect so much as the conceptual diagrams that underlie the work.

After Gehry, who had visualized Boccioni's futurist utopia in matter and space[16], Holl introduced a new view that opened the field to chiasmus, to a spatial interweave. This idea is different from Bilbao, in that it is not a machine that expands in space following urban trajectories or magmatic matter, but rather a process like a ribbon that folds upon itself. The designs of Steven Holl illuminate, with monochromatic colours, this ambiguity of space. The spiral of Wright here transforms into an ascending, deforming path, like a Le-Corbusierian promenade taken to an extreme. Here the space becomes one with the very idea of a traversing. In this museum, which is one of the most interesting projects in recent years, Holl introduces a new alliance between space and memory. Two models, spiral and linear, intermix, but the form of the container is not indifferent to this. On the contrary, it shapes itself to the conformation of the interior space. Memory is thus shaped as an interior place, the space of a Foucaultian heterotopia, of a thousand stories in one. It is an eroded place in which the subject, the interior space, the artistic content and the container shape themselves into a new unity that speaks to us of the cultural and social interweave of our times.

Perception is no longer a unique angle of view, eye-present-past, but a parallel journey, an encounter of cultures, codes, differences.

The space of the Kiasma recounts the latest museum frontier: its projection toward a multiple encounter of souls that dialogue in the imaginary time of emotions.

[1] Regarding the origin of the museum, see Virgilio Vercelloni, *Cronologia del museo*, Jaca Book, Milan 2007.

[2] Regarding Camillo's Teatro della Memoria: Manlio Brusatin, 'Theatrum Mundi Novissimi,' in *Aldo Rossi. Teatro del mondo*, Cluva Libreria Editrice, Venice 1982, pp. 37–8, 47.

[3] On thought machines, see Antonello Marotta, *Daniel Libeskind*, Edilstampa, Rome 2007, pp. 26–41. For those wishing to delve further into the importance of machines in the contemporary age, I also recommend: Edoardo Boncinelli, *L'anima della tecnica*, Rizzoli, Milan 2006; Alexandre Koyré, *Dal mondo del pres-*

sappoco all'universo della precisione, Einaudi, Turin 1967; Vittorio Marchis, *Storia delle macchine. Tre millenni di cultura tecnologica*, Editori Laterza, Rome-Bari 2005; Paolo Rossi, *I filosofi e le macchine 1400-1700*, Feltrinelli, Milan 1962.

[4] On mnemonic devices: Frances Yates, *The art of memory*, Penguin, Harmondsworth 1969.

[5] To understand the phenomenon of the *Wunderkammer*: Horst Bredekamp, *The lure of antiquity and the cult of the machine: the Kunstkammer and the evolution of nature, art and technology*, Markus Wiener, Princeton 1995.

[6] Translation from the Italian: 'Alla privata e soggettiva *Wunderkammer*, il XVI secolo contrappose il salto epistemologico dell'oggettivo *teatro del mondo*, ordinato e sistematico,' Virgilio Vercelloni, *Cronologia del museo*, Jaca Book, Milan 2007, p. 30.

[7] Regarding the evolution of the museum: Maurice Besset, 'Opere, spazi, sguardi,' pp. 12–31 and Ulrike Jehle-Schulte Strathaus, 'La storia dell'architettura dei musei: dal tempio dell'estetica alla fabbrica di informazioni estetiche,' pp. 32–43, in *Museo d'arte e architettura*, Charta, Milan 1992.

[8] In reference to mythology and memory: Károly Kerényi, *Gli dei e gli eroi della Grecia*, Rhein-Verlag AG, Zürich 1958 and il Saggiatore, Milan 1963.

[9] For interesting reading on Marcel Duchamp's ironically titled 1917 work Fountain, his ready-made urinal from a public bathroom, I refer the reader to two works: Bernard Marcadé, *Marcel Duchamp. La vita a credito*, Johan & Levi, Milan 2009; and Janis Mink, *Marcel Duchamp 1887-1968. Art as Anti-Art*, Taschen, Cologne 2000.

[10] Translation from the Italian: 'Prendete un giornale. / Prendete un paio di forbici. / Scegliete nel giornale un articolo della stessa lunghezza che contate di dare alla vostra poesia. / Tagliate l'articolo. / Tagliate poi con cura ognuna delle parole che formano l'articolo e mettetele in un sacchetto. /Agitate dolcemente. / Estraete quindi uno dopo l'altro tutti i ritagli. Copiate coscienziosamente nell'ordine in cui sono usciti dal sacchetto. La poesia vi somiglierà. / Ed eccovi diventato uno scrittore infinitamente originale e di una sensibilità incantevole, benché incompresa dal volgo,' Valerio Magrelli, *Profilo del dada*, Editori Laterza, Rome-Bari 2006, p. 103. In the chapter where he cites Tzara's poem, Magrelli addresses the themes of the metamorphosis of the artistic object and chance as a compositional principle. The volume provides a historical reconstruction of the Dada movement.

[11] For a further review of the themes relating to the Dada phenomenon and their extension to the historical avant-garde movements: Guido Ballo, 'Per l'arte nuova basta dunque la prima idea, la trovata, la proposta?,' in Guido Ballo, *Occhio critico 2. La chiave dell'arte moderna*, Longanesi, Milan 1968, pp. 307–20.

I also refer the reader to a volume providing a meritorious and organic compendium of Dada theatrical texts: *Teatro Dada*, edited by Gian Renzo Morteo and Ippolito Simonis, Einaudi, Turin 1969.

[12] Regarding the museum in the modern era: Luca Basso Peressut, *Il museo moderno. Architettura e museografia da Perret a Kahn*, Edizioni Lybra Immagine, Milan 2005.

[13] Translation from the Italian: 'La funzione primaria assegnata all'architettura del *Centre Pompidou* è pubblicitaria. Questa deve, in primo luogo, catturare l'attenzione dei visitatori potenziali sia *in situ* sia attraverso l'immagine diffusa dai media. Il suo carattere primario è dunque la pregnanza iconica, o più precisamente l'*imageabilité*, il fatto cioè di essere riproducibile, sotto una forma che colpisce, attraverso una copia bidimensionale. Detto in altri termini, è un genere che si rifà all'architettura-segnale e che caratterizza gli agglomerati post-urbani. Nel contesto museologico, questo concetto esprime il privilegio del contenente sul contenuto. Dato che è proprio l'imballaggio, quello che l'industria chiama il "condizionamento," che vincola l'afflusso del pubblico,' Françoise Choay, 'Il museo d'arte oggi: tempio o supermercato della cultura?,' in *QA10, Quaderni del Dipartimento di Progettazione dell'architettura*, Milan 1990.

[14] To read about the museum-city: Alberto Ferlenga, *Aldo Rossi. Deutsches Historisches Museum, Berlino*, Electa, Milan 1990.

[15] Regarding interweave and chiasmus, see Steven Holl, *Parallax*, Princeton Architectural Press, New York 2000. In this volume, the American architect laid the groundwork for his discussion of perception, exploration and the experiential component of architecture.

[16] This theme has been addressed by Antonino Saggio in *Frank O. Gehry. Architetture residuali* (Universale di architettura, Testo&Immagine, Turin 1997). In the chapter titled 'L'atmosfera che circonda le cose,' the author discusses the relations between art and architecture, highlighting the connections between the works of Boccioni from 1911–13, such as *Muscoli in velocità* and *Espansione spiralica di muscoli in movimento*, and those of Gehry, which would culminate in 1997 in his crowning manifesto, the Guggenheim Museum of Bilbao.

Essential

Museums as essential spaces are conceived through a compositional process oriented toward reducing internal complexity and variety in favour of clarity of layout. They are buildings that seek to reunite settings and paths, exhibition spaces and context, into a single whole. The material component is designed to reduce the degree of difference with the surrounding context. The revolution that came about in the first decades of the 20th century, the one of abstractionism triggered by the concrete art of Malevič and extending to Mies van der Rohe's poetics of reduction, generated a deep resonance in this view of museum design. The elimination of ornament, and with it mimetic memory, was the thrust behind these projects, in which the museum recreates elementary, at times hermetic, spaces within the enclosing perimeter and others that are completely transparent to make the building both visually and spatially penetrable.

The different sites, some characterized by interaction with a historical context, others by relationships with parks or landscapes of extraordinary quality, produce diversified designs. But beyond the settings, working with the essential means interpreting the project as an act of removal, of reducing the complex to a few compelling signifiers, in which the site embraces the arrival of the new.

It is a philosophy that seeks to re-establish a priority: simplicity as the essence, as an interrelational void space between inside and out, between museum and city or between museum and the land where it is situated. This paradigm influences everything from the choice of façade to the design of the layout. The structures are often reduced to enclosures, magical spaces, devoid of a citationist intent. Material may be removed or eliminated; the enclosure is still an archetype, mystical, ritual place. These projects invoke silence as a means of conveying drama and remind us that the meaning of the museum is still one of supporting that which is contained within it. In this way, the container is posited as a mediatory element with regard to the city or the park, preventing any schism with the surroundings. The surface becomes a diaphanous field, a lens that often deforms, and things in it appear veiled.

SANAA
Kazuyo Sejima + Ryue
Nishizawa

New Museum of Contemporary Art

2007
New York, New York,
USA

The new museum on Bowery Street in New York's East Village is characterized by its essential yet innovative form. Having a relatively small lot to work with, the design involved using the space in a dynamic and varied way. The museum is composed of seven stacked boxes of different heights and dimensions that are staggered slightly with respect to the vertical axis of the building and generate a neutral exterior faced in a grid of anodized aluminium panels. Thanks to the skewed arrangement of the blocks and openings in the walls, diffused light penetrates into the interior. The interior walls are opaque and act as supports for the works of art. In addition to the exhibition galleries, the museum features a bookshop, a café, a small auditorium in the basement and a multipurpose room on the top floor. The new institution marks an effort to bring new life to a long deteriorated area, uniting the public and private realms in a familiar setting.

SANAA
Kazuyo Sejima + Ryue
Nishizawa

Century Museum of Contemporary Art

2004
Kanazawa, Japan

Lacking a main façade, the ring-shaped museum contains enclosures, essential showcases of memory. Its free and calibrated geometry allows visitors to move through this museum of contemporary art according to its own inner movement. Built in downtown Kanazawa, the museum contains a library, a conference room, facilities for workshops and the exhibition halls. The peripheral, curvilinear windows generate a deformed perspective on the surrounding context and make the interior space immersive and soothing. The glassed-in internal courtyards create a powerful relationship with light, while the galleries, differing in size, offer dynamic and strongly flexible possibilities of path layout. Ancient geometry is reborn in this project, which brings abstraction together with metaphysical space.

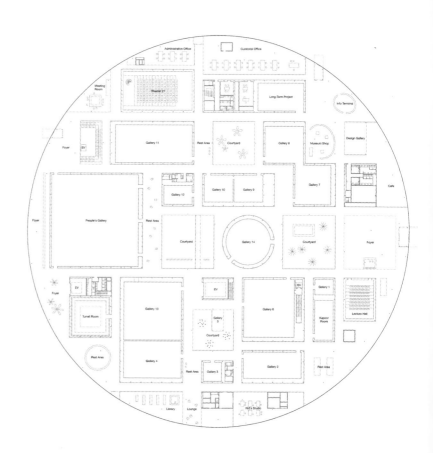

Mansilla + Tuñón
Arquitectos

Royal Collection Museum

2003
Madrid, Spain

This is a project incorporated into an extraordinary framework that is both urban and environmental: the Royal Palace of Madrid and the natural landscape in the western portion of the city. The choice was to design a new volume that would avoid modifying the existing urban spatial equilibrium. This was done by creating a new 'plinth' for the historic building. This makes it invisible from the Plaza de la Almudena, in respect for the historical landscape behind it. Like a containment wall, the new project is conceived as a continuation of the historic structure, with an elementary space marked by the presence of a framework of granite-faced pillars. These generate a measured façade offering a view onto the historical gardens through its sequence of open and filled spaces. The exhibition levels contain three different collections: tapestries, works of art, and historical carriages. The galleries measure 150 × 20 metres. Like a museum-plinth, its spaces are designed to be an optical machine giving outward views of the surroundings.

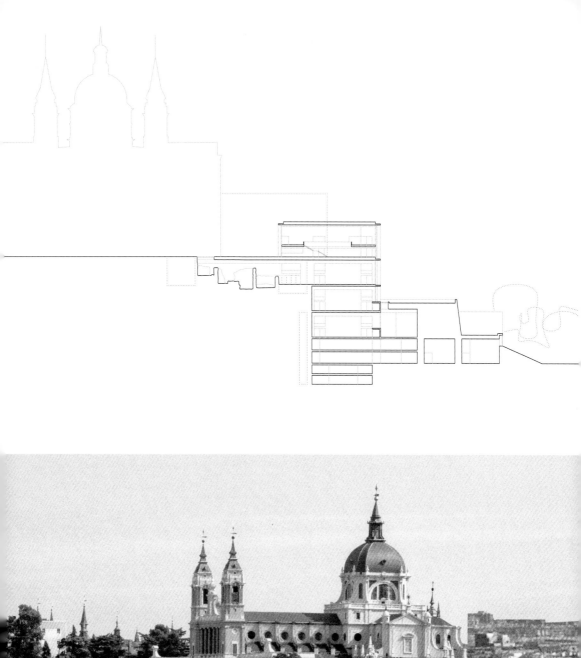

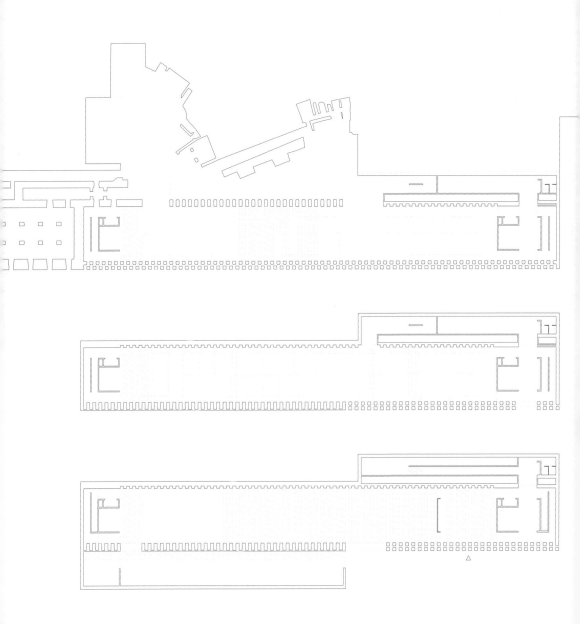

Schweizerisches Landesmuseum Competition

2002
Zurich, Switzerland

The expansion of the Landesmuseum in Zurich is conceived as a new city gate. The building erects a new wall along the River Limmat while the park behind is bordered by another stream, the Sihl. The extension creates a new urban and environmental connection, maintaining continuity with the historical structure. The new wing along the Limmat has been designed to accommodate a conference room, shops and a restaurant on the pier. The project translates into a museum-landscape engaged in a relation with the city. An entrance court located in a node where the old and new structures converge provides access to the respective museums. A tower in the new wing signals the presence of the new institution within the city fabric.

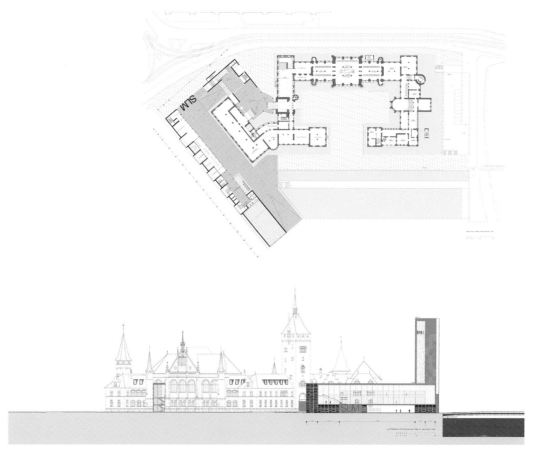

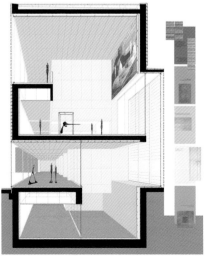

Gigon/Guyer Architekten
Annette Gigon,
Mike Guyer

Kirchner Museum Davos

1992
Davos, Switzerland

The museum in Davos, Switzerland, created in honour of one of the greatest German expressionist artists, is based on the idea of an essential exhibition space outlined by enclosures made of reinforced concrete. It is a museum illuminated by a zenith lighting system. The volumes of the mutually detached galleries generate a composition of regular, autonomous figures interconnected via the circulation system that acts as a spatial binder. In its clarity, it is a museum that translates into a container for art. Externally, this measure and this order are endowed with an abstract power. The construction stands out sharply against the valley behind it and its elementary geometry evokes the abstract period of the 20th-century avant-garde movements, which worked with analogous formal and figural principles.

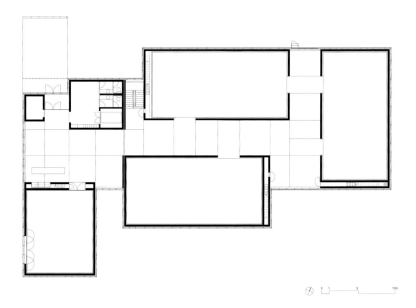

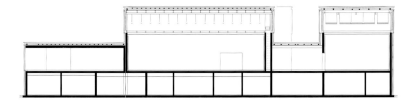

Canary Islands Museum

2003
Las Palmas de Gran
Canaria, Spain

Situated in the Vegueta neighbourhood in Las Palmas, which has witnessed profound changes over time, the museum project seeks to reconstruct an identity associated with the place, an identity of roads, paths and superimpositions. The prevailing idea is the creation of enclosures and small courtyards to generate an internal space composed of interrelations among the parts. The fragmented dimension is resolved through the desire to orient the project around a unitary memory, which necessarily makes reference to the historical city. The museum incorporates itself into an entire city block, conserving the historical façades. It functions through processes of juxtaposition, creating interstitial spaces, voids through which air and light pass. The ground floor accommodates complementary functions while the exhibition spaces are on the floor above. The conference room and the library are accessible from the street and are open to the public. The distance between the old and the new is given material form through a compositional and structural process.

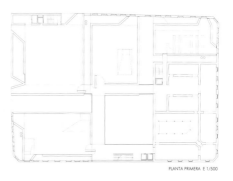

PLANTA PRIMERA E 1/500

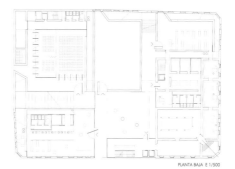

PLANTA BAJA E 1/500

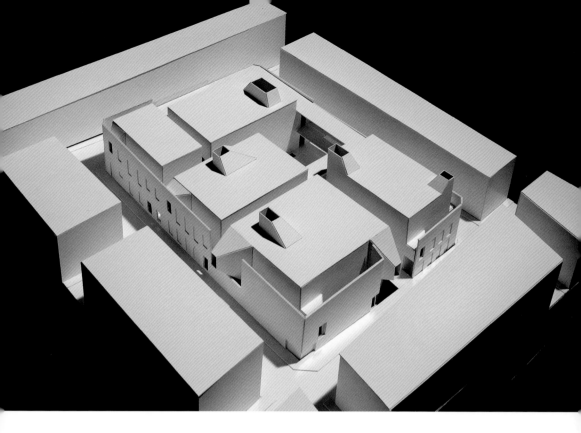

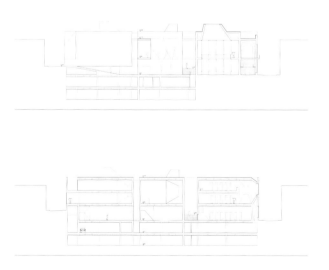

SANAA
Kazuyo Sejima + Ryue
Nishizawa

Glass Pavilion at the Toledo Museum of Art

2006
Toledo, Ohio, USA

The new glass pavilion posits the dual objective of interpreting the materials it exhibits (more than 5,000 glass works produced from ancient times to the present) and reanalyzing the theme of transparency in the transition from the modern era to the contemporary society. Built in a historical park of old-growth oaks, the museum dialogues with and encloses a wooded garden. The exhibition spaces are delimited by glass enclosures, which exclude the idea of separation. It is manifested as an evanescent, ethereal architecture built using the most innovative technologies for glass casting. The curved surface of the glass creates reverberations of light and reflects the trees in the surrounding park. In this need for an expansion of space, the white surfaces of the floors and ceilings generate and reinforce the image of silence and emptiness.

Nagasaki Prefectural Art Museum

2005
Nagasaki, Kyushu,
Japan

The museum is a complex expositional machine in its spatial organization: two units are placed on either side of a canal with water. The interior settings are dynamic and differentiated, and a multivarious range of materials are used. The project is characterized by the strong dialectic between the closure of the stone slabs and the total or screened transparency of the prospects over the waterway. The exhibition galleries are very expansive settings with a great feeling of spaciousness and interrelation with the external context. In its fixtures and finishes, the museum is reminiscent of the backdrops of a stage set. The architect has recovered the culture of the place, the city of Nagasaki, historically a seaport connecting it with the rest of the world. Hence the museum was conceived as an urban connection node, a gateway between the city and the sea: an interface between the inhabitants and the memory of place.

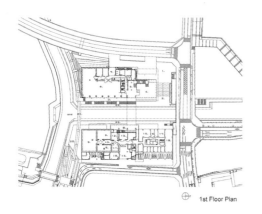

1st Floor Plan

A-A' section

B-B' section

2nd Floor Plan

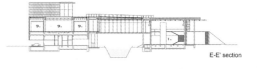

E-E' section

G-G' section

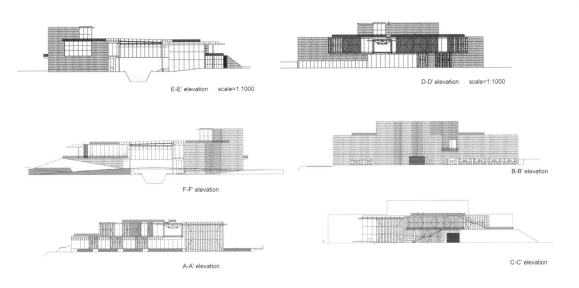

E-E' elevation   scale=1:1000

D-D' elevation   scale=1:1000

F-F' elevation

B-B' elevation

A-A' elevation

C-C' elevation

Tadao Ando Architect
& Associates

Modern Art Museum

2002
Fort Worth, Texas, USA

The museum is conceived as an oasis creating an intense relationship between inside and outside. Built not far from Louis Kahn's Kimbell Art Museum, it seeks a new alliance between the idea of a museum as an essential space and as a landscape. Externally, the regular façade is bracketed laterally by opaque aluminium panels while the centre portion is characterized by the glass wall of the entrance. Inside, one discerns the concept of the new institution from the main atrium: the idea of resting the pavilions over an expanse of water and promoting an aesthetic and contemplative experience in the exhibition galleries that merges with the perception of the works of art. The effect is that of a suspended space. Additionally, the pavilions appear as glassed-in boxes marked by a strongly overhanging roof supported on Y-shaped pillars. The enclosure and transparent qualities are the manifestation of the idea of creating a contemplative setting for art.

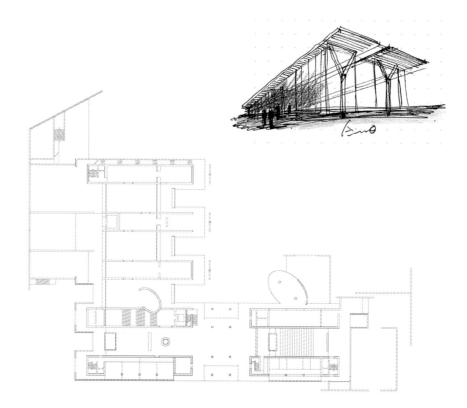

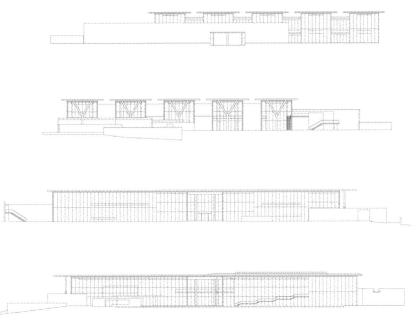

n!studio
Ferrini Stella Architetti
Associati

Conservation Centre for the Museum of European and Mediterranean Civilizations

2005
Marseilles, France

The design competition regarded the redevelopment of the former Muy military barracks in Marseilles and the creation of spaces to be used to store and restore archaeological relics. The project involves the creation of differentiated spaces for visitors and researchers while also modifying the land to establish an urban park. The Centre is imagined as a laboratory where visitors can observe operations. In this project, conserving means communicating the nature of a workshop, a place dedicated to culture. The roofs of the new units fold and deform to create a continuous whole and give the impression of work on a section, a process of erosion. The master plan is resolved with the simple use of the compositional instruments and evokes a way that unites the two- and the three-dimensional, as in Purist painting.

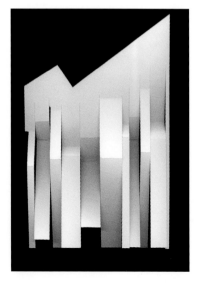

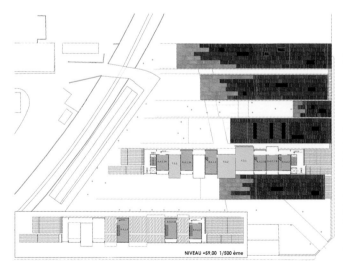

NIVEAU +59,00 1/500 ème

Towada Art Center

2005
Towada, Aomori, Japan

The design competition was called in response to the need to develop the potentials of the city of Towada and its avenue of cherry trees, Kanchogai Street. The proposed plan calls into question the idea of a museum as an enclosed element. It is based on the arrangement of elementary, prefabricated forms which are laid out in an alternation of filled and empty spaces like a chessboard. The design choices evoke Le Corbusier's experience with the Immeubles-Villas in 1922. Here the enclosures carry out a varied structure, in which new relations are created between the exhibition spaces and the outdoor areas, in an interplay of inside and outside. The circulation routes and flows, as well as the exhibition layouts, compose this new relation among the museum's places and spaces. The desire has been to overcome the hierarchical nature of the 19th-century museum and achieve a flexible interpretation within an architectural matrix that still maintains order.

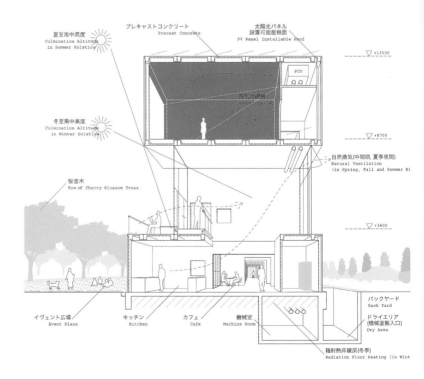

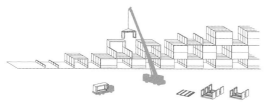

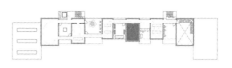

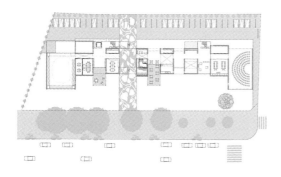

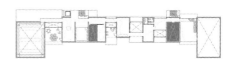

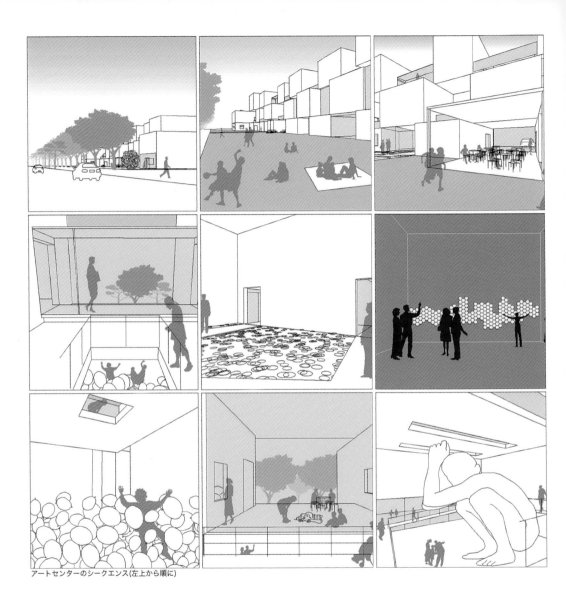

アートセンターのシークエンス(左上から順に)

Monolith

Everything that is solid, enclosed, and impenetrable seeks, first and foremost, to strongly impose its presence in its context. The objective behind this approach when conceiving the design of a museum is to create an immediate relationship with the surrounding reality and, in parallel, to become a new visual pivot point. Materiality often manifests itself as a monolith, a sculptural idea that is enclosed and assertive and does not reveal its inner workings. By withholding legibility, it shifts memory to another level: the museum as a material manifestation seeks to negate the logic of transparency, which in various ways is what generated the democratic thrust of the modern age. The concealment of the internal mechanisms creates a situation whereby we enter a place that needs to be deciphered and comprehended. The projects are often dialectical: that which we would expect to see inside is denied. The spaces are often strongly differentiated. As a consequence, the monolith is an arcane place to be discovered, where the message is received by passing through its material and entering the spaces of its crypts.

It is quite natural that massiveness calls up other identities in one's mind, taking on the guise of a symbol, and the memories evoked necessarily become a recollection of past events, often of a dramatic nature. From this standpoint, matter in itself equates to disquiet, torment and unease. From totemic content to expressive presence, the theme of materiality seeks to affirm the power of enclosure, the transmutation of a conventional substance into one that is self-referential. From stone to aluminium, from reinforced concrete to brick, every material communicates a different sensation and a different message. As a showcase that once made a rite of its languages, in this new conception the museum loses its citationist and iconic component, i.e., its reference to past languages, and often its role as a mere container or place of collection. In this interpretation, which favours impenetrability, even the openings that let in light are called into question. The absence of windows makes the space immediately dramatic. The symbol, as the counter-space to materiality, is grounded in an act of faith, where the exterior denies the interior. The space contained within lives only through discovery and the subject's inner yearning to make out its hidden code.

Ortner & Ortner
Baukunst

MuseumsQuartier

2001
Vienna, Austria

Located within the imperial stables of Fischer von Erlach in Vienna, originally built in 1716, the new museum system is implanted within a Baroque complex, now located within the area of the Ring. It is one of the most extensive projects undertaken within a historical nucleus. The plan involved the insertion of three new units: the Leopold Museum, a cubic white volume faced in limestone evoking a neutral materiality; the Modern Kunst Museum, representing a compact volume in dark basalt with narrow windows; and the Kunsthalle, made of red brick and placed between two pre-existing buildings of the historical structure. The three volumes create a composition of visual and spatial references. The implant marks the presence of the new within the architectural codes of the past and brings new vitality in the form of new public services: food service areas, cafés, shops, bookshops and lounge areas. The project engages with the spaces external to the stables, dominated by the public gardens of the Imperial Palace.

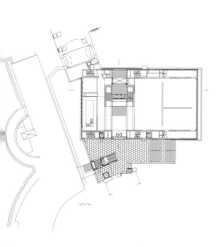

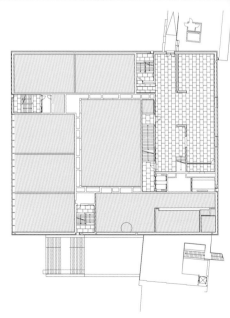

Richard Meier   **J. Paul Getty Center for the Fine Arts**

1997
Los Angeles, California,
USA

Built in the hills of Brentwood above Los Angeles, the new museum incarnates
the idea and form of a contemporary Acropolis. It is a work of vast proportions
evoking an image of massiveness, as if it were a natural outgrowth of the rock.
The arrangement of the buildings leaves space for pools of water and raised
belvederes following the topography of the landscape. The public areas serve
a variety of functions, including reception, open-air performances and theatre.
The five buildings, each one functionally autonomous, contain the auditorium,
information centre, the restoration institute, the museum exhibition spaces and
the art history institute. The buildings are connected via platforms and paths.
Their Travertine marble facing declares a Classical intent and a re-elaboration of
the principles of massive buildings. The topography was carefully studied in order
to enhance the character of the open spaces and to provide an extraordinary
dialogue between the built works and the landscape.

Tod Williams Billie Tsien
and Associates

American Folk Art Museum

2001
New York, New York,
USA

This is one of the projects that most openly declares its material and sculptural intention. On the conceptual level, its 12-metre-wide façade represents the application of pressure to deform broad surfaces. Situated in downtown Manhattan on 53rd Street, it rises like a sculptural monolith, a work by Brancusi in the heart of New York. The exterior is faced in tombasil panels, which are made of a bronze alloy and characterized by a very richly textured surface. Once inside, the museum presents itself very differently, with a complex interplay of planar surfaces and open space that cuts across the entire building. The light illuminating the rooms enters above through skylights. The interior is fitted out with care down to the smallest detail. The narrow floor plan and vertical rise create a composition that maintains a constant tension between the horizontal and the vertical. The museum rewards the visitor with the pleasure of journeying and discovery among different traditions and cultures.

Guillermo Vázquez
Consuegra

Museo Valenciano de la Ilustración

2001
Valencia, Spain

The intervention is incorporated into the triangular area of the Jardines del Hospital in Valencia. Following the demolition in 1974 of the Hospital de los Pobres Innocentes, in 2001 the area was redeveloped and given an archaeological vocation with the introduction of the new museum. Characterized by a bridge-like structure with the crude materiality of unfaced concrete, the building stands as a substantially closed monolith. Its volume is cut by a broad opening leading to the large entrance atrium, which functions as an interconnection node between the two main building units. The space in the atrium is oriented so as to generate a strong sense of emptiness animated by the ramp connecting the various levels. Located in the heart of the historical area, the museum establishes a new boundary between the times, thresholds and characteristics of the historical city and its modern counterpart. It is a work focusing on the archaeological traces and the relation with the empty space left by the demolished historical building.

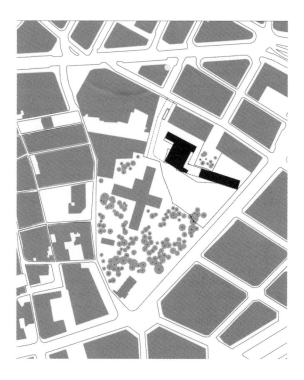

Giovanni Maciocco

Museo del restauro di Sassari

2005
Sassari, Italy

The restoration museum in Sassari is the result of the renovation and transformation of an earlier building that had once been part of a psychiatric complex. Within this context, the museum is an opportunity to ponder the sense of recovering functionality from the pre-existing structure. Ancient and industrial archaeology are combined in a project inserted into a corona of olive trees. The trapezoidal exhibition hall informs the project structurally. It is crossed by a walkway that makes use of the two-storey height. The original brickwork is conserved as a sort of defence of this showcase of memory. In this process of restitching, it is a museum that becomes both subject and object of its purpose. Its compact form places it within the material category, as if to re-evoke, within the enclosure, the origin of the old process of restoration.

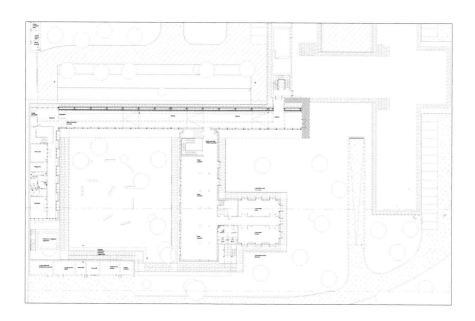

Fine Arts Museum of Castellón

2000
Castellón, Spain

The museum is incorporated into a site characterized by the presence of the historical quadrangular cloister of the Serra Espadá Catholic school. Conceived as a chest closed to the outside, the museum is arranged in four different areas: public areas with exhibition space; semi-public areas with offices; work areas for the Department of Restoration; and lastly, storage facilities and stock rooms. The compact, closed outer shell contrasts with the dynamic and varied interior of the main building thanks to the masterful use and control of lighting. The main unit is composed of five floors and designed to accommodate four permanent collections. The exhibition areas are characterized by a cascade of two-storey open spaces with diagonal circulation flows. Much attention was given to the sections in the design, with staggered floors differentiating and giving character to the various spaces. Finished externally with white cement and aluminium panels, the museum seeks to engage the historical fabric of the area in a dialectical exchange and dialogue.

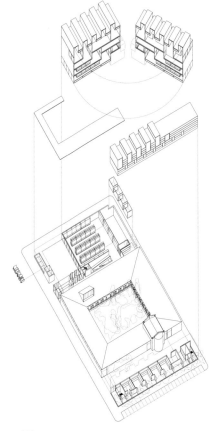

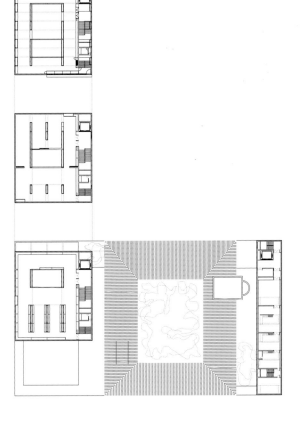

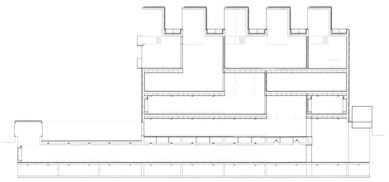

Schaulager – Laurenz Foundation

2003
Münchenstein, Basel,
Switzerland

The museum is designed as a sealed enclosure, an eroded mass that appears to be a storage facility for works of art rather than a distinguished exhibition space. A vertical slice through the building creates a space for intercommunication among the different levels. Externally, the building conveys the image of a huge, symbolic, polygonal monolith. It is an excavated stone, appearing as though extruded from the ground, with horizontal cuts revealing the nature of its material, a granular substance that confers a lithic quality to the whole. It is a work that is both paradoxical and symbolic, thought-inducing regarding the role of memory in the information society and deliberately in contradiction with virtual imagery. The entrance area is characterized by a recess in the building's mass and a small structure with a drum-like roof, a sort of primordial hut reminding us of the origins of architecture.

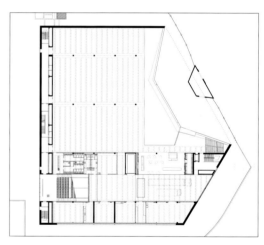

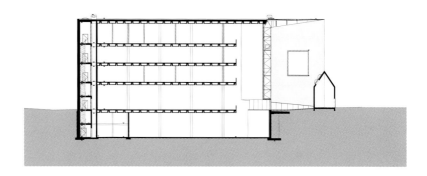

Gigon/Guyer Architekten
Annette Gigon,
Mike Guyer

Museum Liner Appenzell

1998
Appenzell, Switzerland

The museum has a compact yet intricate form. Its façade evokes the image of the historical city and the traditional local houses with a repeating shed roof marking out six exhibition halls which change both in terms of structural rhythm and roof pitch. The goal of this system is to propose a critical regionalism, respond to climatic issues associated with heavy snowfall, and generate a mechanism for capturing light via the sloping roofs. With its external walls faced in chrome steel, the museum communicates a technological materiality, which is partially a statement of autonomy while at the same time re-establishes a contact with the culture of that place, that of the roofs covered with slate. The largest room contains both the entrance and the stairway to the underground spaces. It is a space with a vocation for projecting itself outward through the large window framing the alpine landscape.

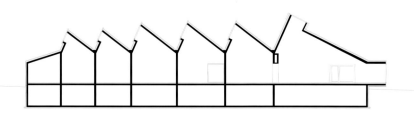

0 1 2   5   10m

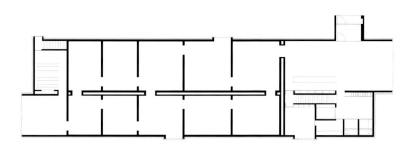

Stone Museum

2000
Nasu, Tochigi, Japan

It is a suggestive project that has grown out of the desire to give new life and functions to the historical granaries in the city of Nasu. These converted spaces are connected via walkways running a few centimetres above the surface of a pool of water, an artificial basin that physically unites the old structures. The paths lead to a plaza on the northern side of the museum, where the exhibition and circulation spaces have been created. The museum draws life from its material existence, from the textures of stone, but it is also clear that the architects have sought to give more emphasis to the void than to solids. They built with the same materials that were used in the granaries: the volcanic rock of Ashino. But this material was worked and arranged in completely different ways to emphasize the differences between the history, technology and culture of the modern with respect to the historical. Here memory is translated into a field of relations.

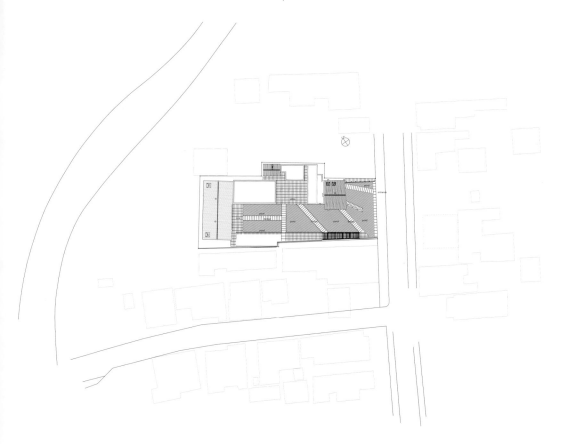

Paulo David   **Arts Centre – Casa Das Mudas**

2004
Calheta, Madeira Island,
Portugal

Perched at the top of a cliff overlooking the Atlantic Ocean, the new Arts Centre
is a block of stone, sculpted following the lines of an abstract geometry
reminiscent of the traditional local architecture and its rocky anchorages.
An eroded platform laid out internally on different topographical levels leads the
visitor into a subterranean experience. A large ramp leads to a square patio, which
in turn provides access to various facilities, all designed to function autonomously
in order to increase the degree of flexibility and possibilities for independent
management. The exhibition areas are located at different elevations and
connected to workshops. The bookshop, adjacent to the patio, functions
completely independently of the rest of the Arts Centre. The library is laid out on
three levels and there is a multipurpose auditorium for theatre, dance, concerts
and conferences. The Centre also features a restaurant on the side overlooking
the ocean. Faced in black basalt, the museum blends into the surrounding natural
landscape.

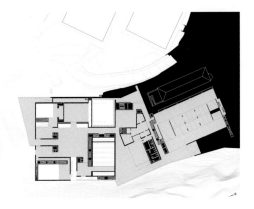 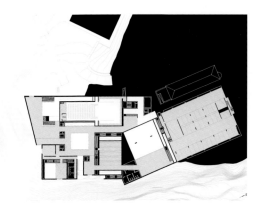

Jiakun Liu

Lu-ye-yuan Stone Sculpture Art Museum

2001
Pi Country, Chengdu,
China

The museum is inserted into a context marked by strong landscape qualities on the banks of the city's river. It is a concrete monolith displaying a crude and brutalist materiality as a response to its purpose as a container for stone sculptures. The museum is accessed via a ramp passing between a bamboo thicket and a pool of water and leading up to the second level entrance. The two-storey atrium is characterized both by the ramp leading up to it and by a walkway connecting the exhibition spaces and service areas. The visit is accomplished by descending from this level. Small fissures and cuts in the building's compact mass open passages for light, which spreads through the exhibition areas like a rain from above. The museum space is projected from the outside in, opening outward again in the sculpture garden on the building's excavated summit. The Lu-ye-yuan Stone Sculpture Art Museum is a convincing building, where material simplicity corresponds to the spatial and compositional arrangement. Appearing closed and dense, the museum maintains a strong connection to the site and the context in which it has been realized.

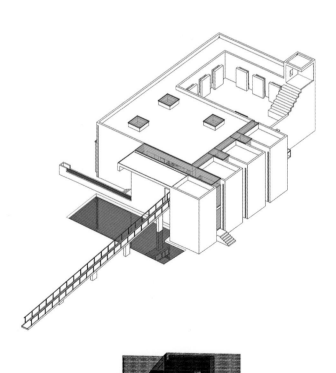

Museum of Automotion

2006
Madrid, Spain

Situated in an area marked by the presence of a motorway and the first public street of Toledo, the Museum of Automotion retraces the history of the automobile and reinterprets the industrial identity of its site. With its autonomous form based on the cylinder, the building is animated within by annular openings in the roof that carve out internal courtyards. The architecture evokes the aesthetics of the automobile. An inclined plane creates a sheltered area that acts as a buffer zone between the indoor exhibition spaces and the outside. The architects carefully designed the building's ability to communicate via materials, using crushed cars that are suggestive of works by Cesar. While the interior is characterized by a simple and essential use of space, the exterior exhibits the plastic nature of the art of wastes, generating new linguistic opportunities.

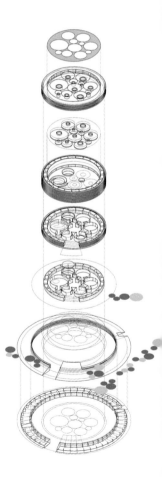

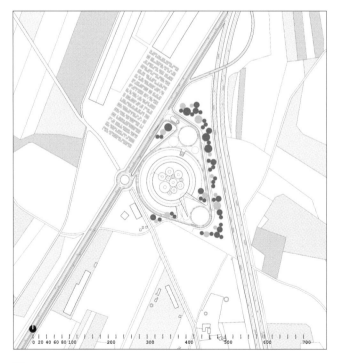

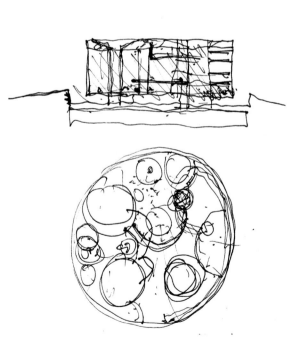

[93] AUTOMOCIÓN

Rudy Ricciotti   **Historial Memorial**

2005
Rivesaltes, France

A new museum serving as a permanent memorial was designed at the Rivesaltes concentration camp to honour the internees imprisoned there. Block F, Camp Maréchal Joffre, was reinterpreted: it had been a refuge for many Spanish republicans fleeing Franco's dictatorship, and in 1942 had become a concentration camp for Jews. Here material encounters the symbol in the form of a space inclined toward the heavens. The museum emerges from the ground just enough to mark its presence. Access to the museum is via a long, narrow tunnel sunk into the ground. This leads to exhibition areas illuminated from above through small openings. Three patios offer spaces for light and air for educational activities, restaurants and offices. The barracks were restored to their 1940 state and bring back to life the feeling of alienation of the imprisonment. This is a place where memory cannot slip away into oblivion. The spontaneous vegetation was extirpated to recreate the desert-like and forlorn, hopeless atmosphere of the camp. Here, in this void brought back to life, the visitor is called upon to reflect on an absurd past.

Daniel Libeskind

Museo Felix Nussbaum

1998
Osnabrück, Germany

The project originated with the idea of creating a home for the works of the artist Felix Nussbaum. It takes form from the interpenetration of three units characterized by different materials: the main unit, faced in oak and containing the foyer and the large exhibition hall; the narrow gallery only two metres wide and eleven metres high, in unfinished concrete; and thirdly the bridge-like connection, faced in zinc, that connects the new museum to its pre-existing counterpart. The most suggestive space is the private gallery, cramped, illuminated by a feeble light entering through a narrow slit in the ceiling. It is a symbolic place that seeks to recount the artist's life, which was filled with continuing periods of exile and wanderings to escape from the Nazis, who would tragically capture him in 1944 in Brussels. The Museum lives off the spatial tension between what the artist has managed to recount in his works and the limited spaces in which he was forced to live during his continuous moves from place to place. The three volumes intersect to create a small private courtyard, triangular in form, a shaded place for thought.

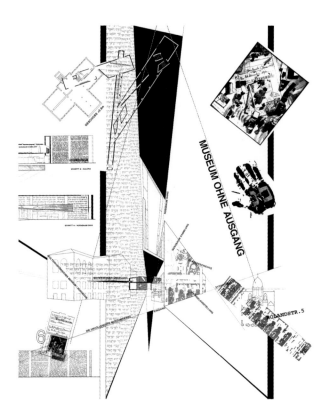

Daniel Libeskind   **Jewish Museum Berlin**

1998
Berlin, Germany

A broken, nervous, diagonal line that recounts the tragedy of the Shoah. The plan takes form from the intersections of lines and trajectories connecting the places where Jewish intellectuals and artists have lived. Connected via an underground passage to the old Berlin Museum, the new project unveils a sense of the void. Laid open inside by large empty spaces, the nothingness creates a place inducing reflection for the visitor. Externally the museum is faced in zinc panels with narrow, dynamic cuts animating the façade. It presents itself as an autonomous container, whose interior cannot be seen or intuited.
A garden dedicated to the poet E.T.A. Hoffmann completes the project. It recounts the forced exile of millions of Jews compelled to abandon their homelands: a mystical place with oleaster trees, the symbol of life, out of reach atop tall pillars.

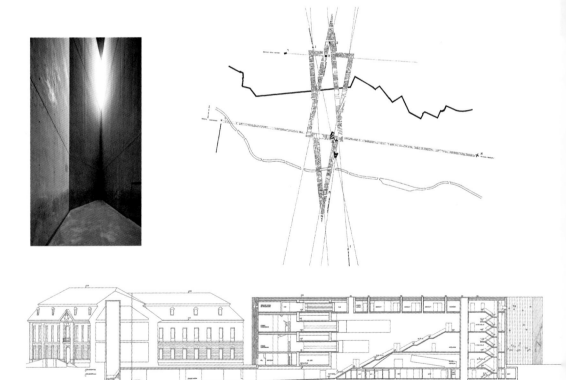

The Museum as Stratigraphic Tension: a story of people and ideas

The interrelationship between archaeology and the museum, between memory and renewal, resolves the indissoluble bond between what has passed and what is projected: on the one hand, accumulated sediment, and on the other, forward vision and an impetus toward the future. When the project forms itself into concrete architecture, it begins a process of becoming ruins, a monument subject to temporal forces, both historical and atmospheric, crystallized by the institutions that generated it and subject to transformation by an energy that slowly consumes it.

This dissolution, this process that leads to the ruin, has oriented architectural culture from the 18th century to the present day with viewpoints and interpretations that change over time.

Travel has offered the possibility to comprehend the lessons of the past. This is the first interpretative path we will analyze in defining the museum as a process of rethinking, as an archaeological act.

Culture has always shifted or expanded its focus to take in the most meaningful places and the monuments that best recount the ancient world. In his *Voyage or a Complete Journey through Italy*, published in 1670, Richard Lassels coined the term 'Grand Tour,' using this locution to describe the idea of movement as a means of enrichment, as the synthesis of the paths and experiences of the places that history has singled out.

It was in the 18th century that a fascination for antiquity was suddenly and strongly rekindled. The archaeological wonders of Herculaneum were discovered during the campaign of excavations initiated in 1738, Paestum came to light in surveys beginning in 1746, and systematic excavation was initiated in Pompeii starting around 1748. These sites—Pompeii arising from its concealing mantle of ash and lapilli and Herculaneum from the once seething mud which had hidden and protected them through the centuries—offered the most intensely emotional visual experience of the past imaginable, risen again from its own ashes.[1]

The architect Mario Gioffredo began reconstruction of the ruins of the ancient temples at Paestum under commission from Charles III of Spain. He utilized the technique of anastylosis, whereby each piece was catalogued and reassembled in its original place. This attention for the reconstruction of the archaeological document *in situ* generated a new way of thinking about the museum as an open space, as a city brought back to light. In his essay *In Ruins*, Christopher Woodward describes with meticulous care the processes of despoliation to which ancient monuments were subjected, with relics ending up in the collections of wealthy aesthetes or worse. As documented in a letter from Raphael to Pope Leo X in 1519, some ancient Roman marbles were actually burnt in order to transform them into lime. This deplorable practice caused the loss of a considerable wealth of historical heritage and speaks volumes about the concern in past centuries for conserving historical treasures.[2] It was not until the 18th century that a new concern emerged for the safeguarding of archaeological sites and relics.

Before the 19th century and the moment the camera began to freeze images of monuments on film, it was the *veduta* artists who kept alive the memory of the past through a slow and painstaking effort of interpretation. The 18th-century etchings of Giambattista Piranesi provided the pleasures of an emotional tale though his hyperrealist technique. The ancient world was no longer interpreted as module or rule—a reading that had marked, in the final analysis, Palladio's work in the eternal city—it was now the pleasures of the narrative that prevailed.

In his etchings done in Paestum in the years 1770–78, shortly before his death, Piranesi showed a passion for those magical spaces of columns and voids, of nature and stone. The prints capture images of fragments and plants that had taken root upon the ancient vestiges. The feeling of nature and the landscape prevailed over the desire to measure the principle of construction. We see a different architecture in Paestum from that recounted in his most famous etchings, *Carceri* [Prisons], begun in 1745 and completed in 1750. In these works the artist captured an image of Rome and its spatiality as an extraordinary constructional machine, resisting through time and richly layered, where we may still see the ribs in the arches and vaults. Throughout his work an image of the sublime prevailed, a sort of gigantism that communicates the theme of the labyrinth. In Piranesi, time became a true *deus ex machina* that replaces the divinity incarnated by the temple and in this annulling any idea of the present.[3]

A connecting thread links Piranesi's thinking to that of the great architect and collector John Soane, who, with his revolutionary project, overcame historical time and entered the contemporary age. He worked as a superintendent in the Bank of England from 1788 to 1833 and continued his archaeological project, designing his factory from within. In an etching by Joseph Gandy (1830), we see it translated into an enormous excavation: a contemporary ruin in which time has reappropriated the walls.

His architectural manifesto and his house at 12 Lincoln's Inn Fields in London represented a dual archaeological project. He lived in this dwelling, now site of the Sir John Soane's Museum, from 1813 to 1837, the year of his death. His passion for collecting led him to accumulate prints, etchings, statues and other ancient memories in his home, which was designed and built with mobile backdrops that revealed the space beyond the setting. In these rooms, the entire past is brought back to life with one relic next to another to generate a place of memory that is like an infinitely layered assembly of strata.

While memory is still accumulation in this dimension, it was Karl Friedrich Schinkel, an architect who was every bit as modern as he was intimately antique, who gave life to an idea of archaeology as selection, as a critical action opening the way to the modern approach. Whereas Roman works, identified with masterfully constructed walls and perimeters, expressed an enclosed and scenographic spatiality, the unearthing of Greek ruins sparked a new interest in light and landscape in virtue of an architecture that rested on punctiform elements. The spatiality evoked through the interrelation of occupied and void space, between the open and the closed, began the interpretation of the museographic project as the staging of a remote identity, of an echo of the settings of the past.

The sketches made by Schinkel in 1804 during a trip to Agrigento reflect his interest in the relationship between the verticality of the columns of the Temple of Concordia and the horizontality of the valley landscape. And so, some twenty years later, something of the cultural dimensions of the *Magna Graecia* found its way into the architecture of the Altes Museum in Berlin (1823–28). Here, by bringing the temple into the museum, the theme of the colonnade is proposed anew, breaking up the sense of enclosed walls.[4] Schinkel had intuited the need to take architecture back to the principles of need, recovering from ancient Greece a sense of tectonics and gravity. He allowed the urban landscape of Berlin to penetrate the dilated wall, the open weave of columns and architraves. Archaeological history became the raw material and very substance of a museum that clearly stated its relation with the city. With Schinkel, the museum projected itself outwards. But its columns conserve, engraved in their deep and fluted shadows, the memory of his journey along the roads of the Achaean colonies of southern Italy. The museum is not merely a showcase that contains, preserves and maintains memory: it is itself an archaeological projection of a dreamt world.

In ruins, where time has erased the stuccowork and decorations, everything is reduced to the tectonic level. Here structure is emphasized and this is what most fascinated that distant generation of architects with their faux pilaster strips and all the rest of their meaningless ornamentation. An example of this approach is contained in Adolf Loos's well known essay *Ornament and Crime*, published in 1908, which opened the way to a modern interpretation of structure. Several years earlier, in 1903, Alois Riegl had published *The Modern Cult of Monuments*, an introductory essay to the revamping of laws regarding historical conservation in Austria, in which the historian's role was to clarify the role of the monument within the historical culture in which it originated and developed. It was a view opposed to the romantic logic of the ruin or that of stylistic and historicist integration and in favour of an idea of conserving a document, meant as a part of the heritage of all of humanity.

At the same time, Loos toppled many previous logical constructs in a battle over the decorative style of the Viennese Secession. It was an extraordinarily vital climate, which witnessed Vienna rallying around a nucleus of writers and artists. The Café Imperial was the meeting grounds not only for Adolf Loos, but also for the expressionist Oskar Kokoschka, the composers Arnold Schönberg and Anton Webern, and the essayist and poet Karl Kraus. These meetings would give birth to new narrative interpretations in various fields of knowledge. In this climate, another famous Austrian, who lived in Vienna until 1938, Sigmund Freud, was penetrating the human psyche, analyzing our dreams as the mirror of our lives. In 1904, he visited the Acropolis in Athens with his brother. He had always been fascinated by the Parthenon as one of the places that evoked for him the settings of the mind, with the soil representing the depths of the subconscious. Like Rome, Athens and its Acropolis was a destination point for intellectuals, writers, and artists who travelled there in a sort of religious pilgrimage to find the hidden meaning of memory. In a letter to Romain Rolland dated 1936, Freud speaks of a *disturbance of memory* caused by the sight of the Acropolis as a *sense of guilt* in seeing something in actual reality that the mind thought only existed in the imagination.

The 20th century rediscovered the world of archaeology, shifting it into an interior space. Back in 1864 in his *Notes from the Underground*, Fëdor Dostoevskij anticipated the Freudian theme of the subconscious with a tale that was a stream of consciousness lacking in any information about the external world. Freud theorized it in 1906 in his *Delusion and Dream in Jensen's Gradiva*, where he proposed an analytical approach to interpreting the inner world, an operation of immersion. He psychoanalyzed a story by the writer Wilhelm Jensen in which an archaeologist, Norbert Hanold, discovers a bas-relief in a Roman museum of a young woman in motion: she touches the ground with only the toes of one foot. This image of lightness triggered a series of timeless fantasies in the scholar. The young and wealthy archaeologist travels to Pompeii to witness his dream in a 'real'[5] experience.

Freud nurtured a passion for archaeology as a metaphor for investigation and analysis via digging and uncovering, removing. After all, both archaeological and psychological research feed on buried memories. Myth thus becomes a field of examination that is open and renewable. The past is translated into a living experience that is still capable of orienting the future. Witness to this great passion is the large collection of over 2000 works of ancient art that Freud left in his home at 20 Maresfield Gardens in London, which became the Freud Museum in 1982. As we are told by Virgilio Vercelloni, the philosopher of the subconscious loved to have these relics around him with the purpose of bringing back an ancient pleasure. He succeeded in saving this private museum when he fled Vienna after the Nazi occupation. Freud loved to change both the order and the placement of the objects, to remind others and himself that memory is not a static thing, but something that is in constant and creative flux.

As a consequence, in this historical phase of the 20th century, the past became a necessarily interpretive field. The great architects of Modernity found the deep purpose of their designs in the journey, which was the occasion for breathing the aura of the past. At the start of the century, while the industrial machines were modifying the nature of the city and the land around it, the architects glimpsed in the pathways of ancient times the possibility to comprehend their own inclinations.

Between 1910 and 1911, Le Corbusier and his companion in study, Auguste Klipstein, made *Le Voyage d'Orient*, a far-reaching tour that would take them to Central Europe, Greece, then Turkey and finally Italy. Le Corbusier visited Athens on this trip, a destination of fundamental significance. He wrote of the experience in these words: 'With my bag on my shoulder,

I travelled by foot, on horseback, by boat or car, beholding the diversity of the races and the substantial equality among men.'[6] Here he discovered the overpowering light of the Mediterranean and was struck by the rural dwellings, the simple objects, the minimal and controlled gestures. In his *Notebooks*, he sketched the Acropolis with the intention, on one hand, of reading the perspectives and relations among the sacred monuments and, on the other, of seeking to render the sensation that the structures which, viewed from afar, almost seemed to form a whole with the sacred mountaintop, as if emerging from its very rock. While the presence of the Parthenon communicated a deep sense of spirituality to him, a *machine that stirs the soul*, like a presage and a quest for his future works, when he visited Villa Adriana in Tivoli in 1911, what fascinated him about this mysterious place was its evident symbiosis between nature and architecture. Here the fragment and the whole coexisted in an interplay of relations between landscape, structure and natural elements. It was a completely innovative encounter between Roman architecture and an imaginative revisitation of Hellenic culture, a struggle between Dionysus and Apollo, between rationalism and irrationalism, enclosure and cavern. In 1911, the German sociologist Georg Simmel dedicated an essay, *The Ruin*, to these themes. In the principle of disintegration of architecture he saw a return to nature. The ruin thus expressed a new unity between the desire of the human spirit to shape the material world and the desire of nature to reappropriate its substances.[7]

This view of architecture would see the development of two other *topoi* among the great architects of the 20th century: the void and tectonics. Let us take a brief look at the work of Mies van der Rohe and Louis Kahn.

While the dimension of the ruin enters Le Corbusier's designs via a reinterpretation of both space and composition, in Mies van der Rohe's work for the Barcelona Pavilion at the 1929 Universal Exposition, Roman space is evoked and dilated. An expositional museum *ante-litteram*, it was conceived as a fluid space, an artificial platform, in a new relation between architecture and nature. The outer walls of the *domus romana*, which led to the garden at the back via a logical and linear sequence, here open onto a plurality of perspectives, and nature appears as a dynamic space, no longer clustered together as in the *horti conclusi* of the houses of Pompeii. Mies introduced the use of glass walls, a sort of filter between inside and outside. This is an intuition whose echo has resounded to the present day. It represents a metaphysical spatiality, that resolves the loss of the direct relationship between the artificial and the natural. The German architect, thanks to the vital encounter with the members of De Stijl and the Suprematists such as Mondrian, Van Doesburg and El Lissitzkij, translated the wall-enclosure into slabs which, losing their archetypical sense of conjoining elements, produce the modern conception of the dilation of space.

When Mies completed the Neue Nationalgalerie in Berlin in 1968, he transposed the structure of the Greek temple into a metallic frame, where structural and spatial clarity reveals a clear classical derivation, united with an allusion to the Turbinenhalle by Peter Behrens. The architect eliminated the regular rhythm of the columns to construct a museum that is a sort of intimate glass showcase, in an interplay between inside and out. From inside the gallery one perceives the external space indirectly, via the line of shadow of the deep, overhanging roof, generating a dimension of mystery such as that which marked the passage from light to shadow in Eleusinian rites.

More than any other architect, Louis Kahn has succeeded in forging the space of the museum in an alliance between matter, structure and archaeology. When he built the Kimbell Art Museum in Fort Worth, Texas in 1967–72, he thought of it as a sequence of rooms with apparently simple and serially repeating spaces which escape their configuration as the visitor crosses through them. The Kimbell was before its time. It is a suspended space, shaped by light, in which the visitor moves from the internal exhibition spaces to outdoor areas conceived as another museum in an intimate relation with the landscape. Here the myths of the past re-emerge: the lessons received from visits to the Pantheon, Trajan's Market and the Villa Adriana provide a special viewpoint on the ancient world. Kahn thus begins a quest starting with the Roman ruins, identifying in that history the sense of the building's tectonics. The museum imposes its material presence just like its historical counterpart with platonic forms and pure geometries. It takes a double lesson from the ruins: on the one hand, the material stripped bare in which the undecorated walls communicate their structural power, on the other, the symbolic charge that such works evoke in the observer.

Having gone beyond the still mimetic interpretation of the 19th century, wholly centred on architectonic registers and respectful of grammatical semantics, memory witnessed an extraordinary reinterpretation with the 20th century. It is not just the theme of utopia or abstraction as much as the capacity to recover past relations rather than merely their representation. Thus, of archaeological ruins, Le Corbusier, Mies van der Rohe and Louis Kahn reinterpreted, respectively, space, removal and tectonics. The museum entered a private and complex, certainly personal universe. In this stage the architect sees history as a source of inspiration, a search engine, and rarely stoops to imitation.[8]

Hence, in the 20th century, modern architecture brought back the archaeological dimension as a founding part of museum design and, as an extension, of urban design. The many trips to the source territories of the ancient world communicate to the architect the sensations and principles for reordering their compositional material. When the axis shifts away from the theme of structure, space and matter and is reflected in the horizontal plane of the traces and signs of history, the theme of memory takes on the hues of immediate relations and the archaeological city, in its various strata, enters into a strong dialectic with the modern city. We enter an interpretation of archaeology as an ordering path, a network of relations, a redefinition of the limits.

In the mid-1960s a new current came into being that saw in theoretical research the answer to a series of questions regarding the relation between history, city and territory. In 1966 two books that would constitute a central point in the discussion on the ancient and modern city and the identity of place were published: *L'architettura della città* by Aldo Rossi and

Il territorio dell'architettura by Vittorio Gregotti. That same year, Robert Venturi had opened the way to interference by the media in spatial form with his *Complexity and Contradiction in Architecture*.

While international culture toward the close of the 1960s on the one hand turned its attention to structural experimentation and a machinistic utopia (take for example the Metabolists in Japan or the Archigram in England), in Italy theoretical research was oriented toward recovering signs of the past, where history and geography redefined the limits of the design-oriented pursuit.

In the 1970s, the international debate on architecture identified the central driving forces in archaeological recovery and in the museumification of places that have conditioned memory from time immemorial: Athens and Rome. The great design competitions were what was supposed to give an answer to the fates of places that were so well documented, so powerful as to make the designs seem obsolete right from the moment they were proposed.

Regarding Rome, in the 1980s the group Benevolo-Gregotti elaborated the *Study for the arrangement of the central archaeological area* (1985). Gregotti and Benevolo's project provided a sort of resolution: on the one hand, the large scale of the project and, on the other, a topographical and structural reconstruction involving the pre-existing archaeological elements and the urban context that had been established in the immediate vicinity. The solution was to work underground, creating a subsurface museum. Regarding the museum for the Acropolis in Athens, won by the studio Passerelli in a 1989 design competition, the solution was a large project that was like a platform gazing upon the past. However, the fact of the matter is that the implications of those places were too strong and the proposals remained for two decades on paper.

Rome and Athens not only represented the central pivot points of the history of architecture, but the question of a museum project in these places opened up a host of daunting issues since intervening in their memories meant necessarily modifying them.

The relation between the museum and archaeology did not address so much the relic or unearthed fragment as it did the signs, the geometry, the traced routes and the interweaves that constitute the underpinnings of the ancient city, its very inner structure. Having gone beyond the 1980s and the theme of the fragment which recorded and exalted a crisis that affected the very meaning of the architectural project, archaeology attempted to clarify its deepest and most ancient strata. Yannis Tsiomis, one of the preeminent scholars in the relation between museum design and archaeology, clarified the need to comprehend the thresholds and the limits that separate the past from the present. In the project to create a museum in the Agora of Athens (1997–2001), Tsiomis overturned the vantage point: now it is the modern city that makes itself flexible so it can take in its ancient counterpart in a relation of reciprocity. This meant rethinking relations, customs and functions that connect the two systems. The limit addressed by Tsiomis is not merely physical but also cultural: it is our capacity to restore life to the past. This is a central shift in the contemporary archaeological viewpoint, having seen the various operations in the past that attempted to isolate the historic heritage by moving it away from the life of the city.

Paul Valéry was one of the first to intuit this limit with the publication, on 4 April 1923 in the magazine *Le Gaulois*, of his text *Le problème des musées*, where he fought against the very idea of a museum as a space that takes in dead matter. The poet considered senseless the thinking that would separate a thing, which originated in a specific historical and geographical setting, from its context. History unfolds in an evolutionary relationship and the city is endowed with multiple layers that accumulate in the same place over time. In this interval, the archaeologist's work cannot give us back the past as it once was. Let it suffice to think of the reconstructed Parthenon and the image, marred by a number of fallacious details, communicated to the visitor.

In this accumulation of strata that is the contemporary city, some strata are visible and others are completely hidden. The difficulty in the archaeological project originates in this reading of the stratified city. Subject as it is to gaps and fractures that have marked it over the centuries, the urban body does not necessarily represent a continuous whole.

After the 1970s—when post-structuralist philosophy cast light on thousands of levels of spatial and human nature, lacking any well delineated territory or reconciliation—talking about the past meant encountering memory that does not subsist on continuity, but rather one that contends with discontinuity and, most of all, the void. The trace is no longer the objective venue of history, but rather a dynamic space that must be rewritten using new figures.

We enter the recent view that sees archaeology as a lacuna. Let us look at a few interpretive passages. What is a trace?

In 1930, the philosopher Ernst Bloch published the book *Spuren* [*Traces*], a series of fabulist stories in which he introduced the theme of thinking in traces and the method of seeking out clues for missing or overlooked details. It was an approach that came to maturity in the 1930s in the atmosphere of German expressionism, against Nazi ideology which had adversaries in—as well as Ernst Bloch—Walter Benjamin, Bertolt Brecht and Siegfried Kracauer. Bloch developed a narrative intended as a combinatory art against a backdrop of the popular fairy tale, an uncontaminated world which, being a myth, was open, in which the text does not follow the linear principle of the development of the tale, but is interrupted by doors and frames that allow conceptual leaps, openings onto other systems like entrances and exits, the going away and coming back. The aim was to penetrate the world of the irrational, in which movement is broken up, either retracing its steps or following unpredictable traces. This narrative, which drew existence from 'temporal passages' was the response to repression of the mind. The expressionist and surrealist climate generated an amnesia, a loss of memory, in order to create another way of seeing reality.

In his book *Grammars of Creation*, George Steiner points to the end of a classical aesthetics searching for fullness starting with Mallarmé's game of blank spaces in texts. From there we enter the abstract painting of Kandinskij, the compositions of Schönberg with their dissonances and silences, Giacometti's sculptures, denuding matter to leave it stark, and the writings of Beckett, in which the wait becomes the narrative substance of the void. The issue to which they were seeking a response in this phase of the 20ᵗʰ century was how to interpret history, how to analyze the present, how to offer an alternative to a totalitarian viewpoint.

Michel Foucault proffered an answer in 1969 with *The Archaeology of Knowledge*. The philosopher focused his interpretation on the overcoming of an idea of history as a continuous movement: '[…] the problem is no longer one of tradition, of tracing a line, but one of division, of limits; it is no longer one of lasting foundations, but one of transformations that serve as new foundations, the rebuilding of foundations.'[9] He analyzed a history of thought as a discontinuity, while that which is conventionally understood omitted the *irruption of events*. The multiplication of strata, of differences, shatters the idea of the cyclicality of historical events, an idea born of a view of progress and the goal of reason that was still positivist. The strata of history 'overlap and intersect without one being able to reduce them to a linear schema.'[10] It was a view that turned on its head the general model that *progresses and remembers*. It was not a question of creating a separate history, but rather—through the analysis of the *series, spans, limits, gaps* and *scraps* that compose the complex scenario of life—of seeking out the connections among the different analyzed areas. This realization seeks to call into question the certainty that everything fits into a predetermined schema. Like Ernst Bloch before him, Foucault denied a conception of the past based on rationality.

History has proven to be a material that is alive and in tension. The Hegelian concept of a continuous progression, like the development of a spiral whereby events tended toward a sort of evolutionary cycle, is negated by historical facts. Sometime around 1450 BCE, Mycenaean culture, much less evolved than its Cretan counterpart, wiped out the more advanced aesthetic and technological knowledge that once belonged to the civilization of the Palace of Knossos.

With *The Archaeology of Knowledge*, Michel Foucault called into discussion the structure of scientific knowledge—unidirectional, structural, associated with an unambiguous power—and invoked the differences, the palimpsests, the polysemous multitudes of signifiers. The philosopher introduced a new stratified idea of the individual, no longer subjected to a single social utopia but undeniably interacting within a stream of possibilities, in a collective heterotopia. This view is recounted through accumulation, excavation, gaps, radiographs.

It was art that allowed us to penetrate into this dimension. Francis Bacon introduced us into the space of accumulation. A famous photograph portrays him sitting in his studio, thinking, lost in his distorted world, in tension, tragic. There is a narrow path leading to the canvas through the great quantities of refuse the artist had accumulated in a time with no coordinates, a warning of unease, scraps understood as social exclusion.

Stratification lives in the work of Mimmo Rotella. Through his ripped posters remounted on canvas that he then modified with the rules of chance, he invited us to see the city as a heterogeneous whole composed of information. While Robert Rauschenberg, with his series *Combine Painting* incorporating various objects into a painted canvas surface, hinted at a complex interweave of ancient and contemporary references.

The contemporary age, after having gone through the Post-modern period in the late-1970s and 1980s, which looked into a mirror to reinterpret history and tame it, make it a household thing, now recriminates its archaeological dimension. Hence the stratigraphic interpretation implies that history cannot be taken to be a process of selection, of isolation of one phase with respect to another, but rather a process of overlapping through time. This is a metaphor that brings to mind the layers and strata of a mountain, in which heterogeneous materials have accumulated. In this conception, the excavation becomes the process by which architecture re-establishes contact with the foundational act.

It was the Basque sculptor Eduardo Chillida with his project for the Tindaya Mountain on Fuerteventura in the Canary Islands (1996) who introduced us into a contemporary cavern. It communicates a mystic and scabrous message with its weathering steel, where reflected light penetrates asymmetrically through skylights. It is a buried cube measuring approximately 50 metres per side. The excavation is translated into a void, where the box is missing, a complex space that has always carried multiple architectural meanings. The action of the project began with eliminating material through its foundation. By means of the excavation as a constructive process, architecture becomes conceptually closer to archaeology. This is taken as a descent into the depths, as a place of unease, as the space of our inner memory.

The place of relics has always invited us into an intense interior dialogue. We enter the space of symbols, memories, senses of belonging. The symbol reminds us that there was time before us, it lets us know that a past exists, and it offers us the gift of a future idea. Time, as the paradigm or material of architecture, assumes in this perspective a parallel identity. The museum, place of the sediments of memory, leads us into a dimension that is renewal, tension, change.

But archaeology exists not just as materiality, but more deeply as a void, a loss or erasure. In 1926, poet Federico García Lorca in his *Ode to Salvador Dalí* wrote 'you love the architecture that builds on the absent.'[11] The void is the lacuna, the space in which we reconstruct our past, projected forwards. But this implies the need to interpret the body of the city and, at the same time, to get an x-ray of the body social, to succeed in seeing our inner nature.

One of the most intense moments in this regard involved Dalí. In 1859, the artist Jean-François Millet painted a work titled *The Angelus*. It portrays a rural couple with their heads lowered staring, with an unutterable soul-felt pain, at the ground. Critics saw a symbolic character in this representation associated with the fertility of crops; a bond with the material culture of the earth. This intimate relation, which here is translated into anxiousness and pain, was perceived by Salvador Dalí as a substance to be excavated, unveiled, understood. The Catalan artist perceived a hidden, cryptic element in that work. He suggested to the director of the museum that the painting, kept in the Louvre, should be subjected to x-ray analysis. He intuited that there was something buried under the mound of earth. The study revealed that Millet had painted over a small coffin containing the farmer's dead child. The reasons for his choice were dictated at the time by a lack of interest in the theme of the ritual or the tragic. But with this concealment, the painting, hiding the mechanisms that had caused the tragic event, enters a new, complex and unexpected dimension. In 1935, Dalí painted a new version titled *Archaeological Reminiscence of Millet's Angelus*, in which the two figures have been transformed into ruins, like a surreal archaeological memory, like matter capable of consuming itself. The woman, bearing the greatest pain, is the most anguished figure in Dalí's composition.

The theme of forgetting, of oblivion, of erased space, of that which is concealed from our memory brings us onto a path in which existence lives in this absent space. It was Cesare Brandi, in his *Teoria del restauro*, who identified the full problematic extent of the lacuna, as a place in which the present reflects on the past.[12] In this view we pass from a field that was considered objective to one that is process-driven and interpretive. Within this stratification even memory cannot be frozen but demands a new interpretation.

Hence the idea of the lacuna changes with time. It transforms in the passage from Modernity, in which it represented the space of rewriting, to Post-modernity, the contradictory space, in which it inquires about loss and erasure. As a consequence, the lacunae and oblivion are the spaces of contemporary archaeology. Visible and invisible—the categories that the philosopher Merleau-Ponty chooses to reinterpret this age—reconcile the plan of the city from the archaeological plan hidden from sight. The loss of information thus touches the monument, but even more deeply the city.

If we usually think of the realm of traces as the space of sedimented memory, as the visible signs of a heroic past, and again as the ruins that bind us to romantic reminiscence where things come back in a slow fade-in to their natural state, at the same time, by means of the unresolved texts of our contemporary era, we encounter other ruins, other detritus. It is the space that the sociologist Marc Augé invites us to enter in describing the remains of the Berlin Wall, as the tale of an archaeological substance in the modern day. In one passage the author claims: 'History is also violence, and oftentimes the spaces of the large city receive the full impact of the blow and bear its wounds. This vulnerability and this memory resemble those of the human body, and are doubtlessly what makes the city feel so close, so exciting to us.'[13] The city as an archaeological place reflects like a shadow on the destinies of the peoples who live there. Berlin, as writes Emmanuel Terray, is the *paradise of shadows*, the realm of the great contradictions and of the wounds of the madness of the 20th century. This matter was interpreted by Paul Virilio in his text *Bunker Archaeology* (1994).

The French philosopher interprets the painful past with the eyes of Foucault and invites us to observe a reality of war, reinforced concrete buildings from the Second World War planted in areas of extraordinary beauty, like expressive architectures that evoke the admirable works of the German architect Erich Mendelsohn. It was the paradox of associating, in a photographic journey through contemporary memory, military cement with its noble, existential counterpart, the free, tensioned, revolutionary work of the great expressionist artist of the Einstein Tower.[14]

Thus the allusions obsessively return in which architecture reacquires an opaque, material dimension by eliminating material through a process of subtraction. In his text *Architecture Without Architects* published in 1964, the historian Bernard Rudofsky addresses examples of structures originally built as substructions, dug into the rock via the slow action of the elements or where humans have shaped the mountain by penetrating into its interior as if into a maternal womb. These are enduring works, bound to their place, transformed or consumed by the wind, in which nature and artifice coexist to the point where their differences are lost. These territories now re-emerge in the tensioned spaces of the new museums.

In the 1990s, architecture began to explore the realm of the underground and its 'memories' through the shaping of the land, the folds of Deleuzian conception, which excavates space as does existence. Manipulating the land means encountering the shapeless cavities of the caverns, the pre-classical underground realms. This period has led architecture back into a subconscious space, into a regressed memory—an archaeological memory—whence history starts again.

[1] For an overview of themes: Ranuccio Bianchi Bandinelli, *Introduzione all'archeologia*, Editori Laterza, Rome-Bari 2004. For a historical and archaeological reconstruction of the Pompeii and Herculaneum sites, which did much to modify both aesthetic and architectural history from then on, I recommend two important texts by the archaeologist Maiuri: Amedeo Maiuri, *Pompei*, Istituto Poligrafico dello Stato, Rome 1978; and Amedeo Maiuri, *Pompei ed Ercolano fra case e abitanti*, Giunti Editore, Florence 1983.
I also mention a text that has the virtue of presenting a comparative reading of archaeological literature and contemporary art: Ranuccio Bianchi Bandinelli, *Organicità e astrazione* [1956], Electa, Milan 2005.

[2] For an analysis of ancient times: Christopher Woodward, *In ruins*, Vintage, London 2002.

[3] For an understanding of Piranesi's works: Luigi Ficacci, *Giovanni Battista Piranesi*, Taschen, Rome 2000. The artist's oeuvre has been reinterpreted by critics as a prediction of the future. Manfredi Tafuri wrote in 1973: 'But the Prisons, precisely because they are infinite, coincide with the space of human existence. The hermetic scenes drawn by Piranesi, in the weave of his "impossible" compositions, indicate this with extreme clarity. This means that in the Prisons we can see nothing but the new existential condition of the collectivity, at once liberated and damned by its very reason. And that which Piranesi translates into images is not so much a reactionary criticism of the social promises of illuminism but a lucid prediction of that which a society would be when liberated from ancient values and consequently from the constraints they impose. [...] In Piranesi, the experience of angst makes its first appearance in modern form. In the Prisons, we are already in the presence of an angst generated by the anonymity of the subject and by the "silence of things".' From: Manfredo Tafuri, *Progetto e utopia* [1973], Editori Laterza, Rome-Bari 2007, p. 21.

[4] For further information on the cultural climate in which Neoclassicism was born and developed, see John Summerson, *The classical language of architecture*, The MIT Press, Cambridge 1963.

[5] For further investigations of the relationship between excavation and the mind: Fëdor Dostoevskij, *Notes from the underground and the gambler* [1864], Oxford University Press, New York 1991; Sigmund Freud, *Der Wahn und die Träume in Wilhelm Jensens 'Gradiva,'* in *Schriften zur angewandten Seelenkunde*, vol. I, Heller, Leipzig-Wien 1907. I also suggest: Sigmund Freud, *Un disturbo della memoria sull'Acropoli: lettera aperta a Romain Rolland*, *Opere*, vol. XI, Bollati Boringhieri, Turin 1979.

[6] Translation from the Italian: 'Sacco in spalla, mi muovevo a piedi, a cavallo, in barca, in auto, confrontando le diversità delle razze e la sostanziale uguaglianza degli uomini.' Jean Jenger, *Le Corbusier. L'architettura come armonia*, Universale Electa/Gallimard, Trieste 1997, p. 27.

[7] To understand the thought of this German sociologist better, see the reading of: Georg Simmel, *Frammento sulla libertà*, Armando Editore, Rome 2009.

[8] To extend the comprehension of the connection between modern project and archaeology regarding the past and the travels of modern masters, see Alberto Ustárroz, *La lección de las ruinas. Presencia del pensamiento griego y del pensamiento romano en la arquitectura*, Arquíthesis 1, Fundación Caja de Arquitectos, Barcelona 1997.

[9] Michel Foucault, *The Archaeology of Knowledge*, translated by Alan Sheridan Smith, Routledge, London 2007, p. 6.

[10] *Ibid.*, p. 9.

[11] García Lorca, *Tutte le poesie*, vol. II, Newton, Rome 1993, p. 243.

[12] Regarding lacunae: Cesare Brandi, *Teoria del restauro*, Einuadi, Turin 1977.

[13] Translation from the Italian: 'La storia è anche violenza, e spesso lo spazio della grande città ne riceve in pieno i colpi e porta il segno delle ferite. Questa vulnerabilità e questa memoria somigliano a quelle del corpo umano, e sono indubbiamente esse che ci fanno sentire la città così vicina, così emozionante.' Marc Augé, *Rovine e macerie. Il senso del tempo*, Bollati Boringhieri, Turin 2004, p. 106 (Marc Augé, *Le temps en ruines*, Galilée, Paris 2003). In the chapter 'Il tempo e la storia,' the French sociologist offers us an important thought: 'While everything contributes to making us believe that history has ended and the world is all a show in which that end is acted out, we need to find time to believe in history once again. This might now be the pedagogical vocation of the ruins,' p. 43.

[14] Regarding the new places of memory: Paul Virilio, *Bunker Archaeology*, Princeton Architectural Press, New York 1994.

Archaeological

In the contemporary age, archaeology presents a substance that is still capable of providing food for thought regarding our future. Archaeological materials, composed of strata unearthed through excavations into the past, make it possible for us to stay our course through a space characterized by dwindling reference points. And when this is the very profound essence addressed, the museum cannot help being evocative: it is metaphorical by nature, it calls to mind the theme of origins. Its substance touches on the grand duration of time. As something whose vocation is to resist the passage of time, it communicates a sense of stability.

The literature of projects is not uniform; some quests exhibit their diversity. In some cases the museum is a sort of impenetrable showcase evoking the unbreachable temporal divide between the past and the present. In others, the tension between archaeological layers is etched into the surfaces of the museum, which bear witness to the stratifications of time. The design may also seek the role of container providing shelter to preserve an archaeological site, or—and this is the most interesting situation—create a sedimented landscape, one that is itself archaeological, like an ancient platform. What is witnessed in the recent literature is a paradigm shift whereby the museum invokes the theme of penetrability or passage. It becomes a gateway between superimposed histories, between the histories of ancient places and the contemporary cities. Here the selection and categorization processes typical of nineteenth-century culture have been replaced with an idea of a mutual presence of periods and cultures. A museum that addresses a bygone era cannot be an acritical container: it demands review, reinterpretation. Thinking about this means coming into contact with the themes of continuity and rupture, respecting all developments that have been an integral part of the history of a city and its lands. In this sense, the museum sublimates its substance when it evokes our analytical capacity to dig into our identities. Archaeology, as a consequence, touches on the theme of the void, of the material removed to bring the relics back to light. Its structure lives for its internal spaces, rarely does it open to the outside. In this instance, memory is the quest for a private space, a flow of consciousness that enters our minds from outside, in an indefinite space that we call existence.

Archaeological Museum of Almería

2004
Almería, Spain

The context for the new museum project, surrounded by buildings of notable height, conditioned the choice of a compact volume. The museum is accessed via an area complementing the urban fabric: an open plaza with palm trees. It is configured as a public space, open to the city. The museum building is characterized by a hermetic exterior with broad surfaces of Almería marble. The openings and arrangement of the marble slabs evoke a memory of the archaeological excavation and its strata. Enclosed within is a luminous interior composed around a large central void. This internal hall unites the various levels, orienting the visitor and connecting the exhibition halls of the archaeological collection. Large windows open onto external views at special points along the path. The intense zenith lighting is controlled by a screening system made of okumè wood.

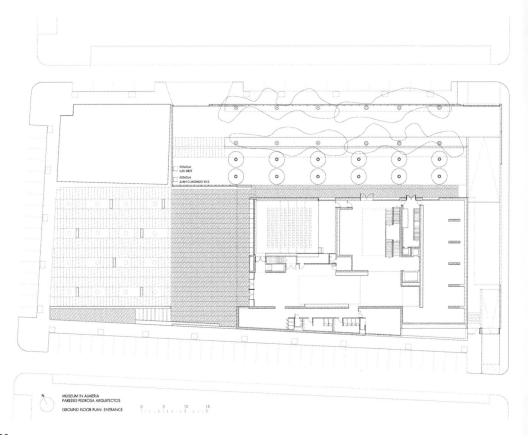

MUSEUM IN ALMERIA
PAREDES PEDROSA ARQUITECTOS
GROUND FLOOR PLAN. ENTRANCE

0   5   10   15

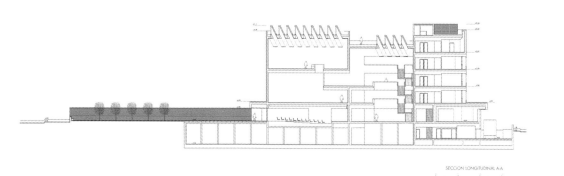

SECCION LONGITUDINAL A.A

Provincial Museum of Zamora

1996
Zamora, Spain

Built near Plaza de Santa Lucía in the historical centre of Zamora, the museum is a showcase for the city's memories. The exterior is faced in well positioned bricks and does not manifest itself as a true façade, an identity which is denied by the near total absence of openings. The true face of the museum is the rooftop, which transforms into a variegated façade of skylights that create a pattern of differing forms, heights and textures. The museum can be seen from above from a road that climbs the ridge. Built in a void, characterized by a series of topographical incidents, the building denies any axial composition and manifests itself as an interstitial space in relation to the other buildings among which it is nestled. A rock wall acts as a backdrop to its compact and durable volume. Inside, void space and simple walls in white stuccoed concrete are the prevalent characterizing elements. Light streaming down from above contributes the magic of this sheltered showcase.

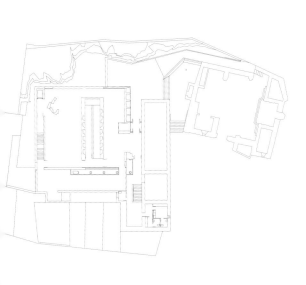

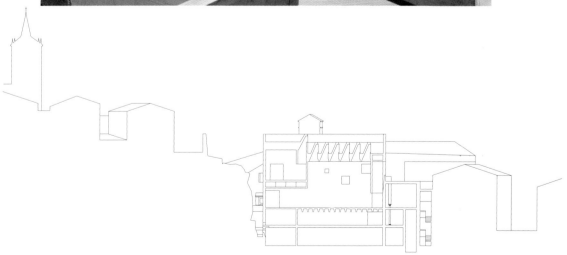

Giovanni Maciocco   **Museo Archeologico Nazionale di Olbia**

2007
Olbia, Italy

Located on a small islet off the northern portion of the Olbia coast, the archaeological museum has been built around an early twentieth-century building. A small bridge connects the museum to the mainland. Conceived as a medieval village engaged in dialogue with the sea, the building has a dual nature of slab and mass juxtaposed in an interchangeable relationship. A large drum-like structure rises from the complex stating its function as a generative element around which the entire composition rotates. The museum grew out of the need to provide a response to a land rich in history and ready to accommodate the monumental relics recovered from Roman and medieval shipwrecks. Its external guise is that of a citadel of culture. Inside, the pre-existing building is rotated with respect to the main axis and a large courtyard reminiscent of Sironi's metaphysical landscapes allows the visitor to grasp the spatial relations of the interior. The interstitial spaces between the curved wall of the façade and the circular space of the drum are particularly impressive.

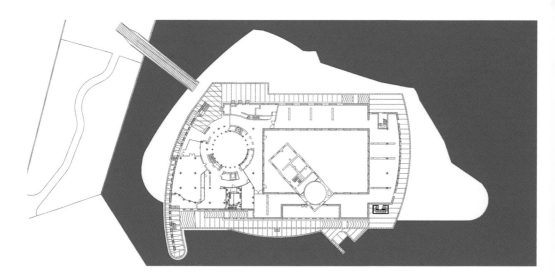

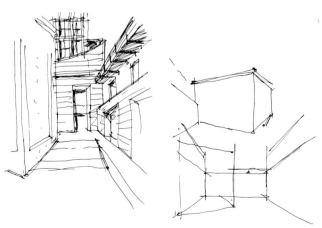

Bernard Tschumi
Architects

New Acropolis Museum

2009
Athens, Greece

Built on one of the earth's most extraordinary sites, at the foot of the Acropolis, the new project seeks to recover certain principles from Greek archaeology, such as the relationship between the building and the void space around it, the geometrical/mathematical clarity of form, and the idea of designing a museum that would represent a sort of forward position toward the city.

The base of the museum is a two-storey trapezoid containing the archaic period galleries. The building is supported on pylons in order to allow work on the Makriyianni archaeological excavations to continue. They are accessed from the entrance atrium, which also leads to the temporary exhibition areas. A rectangular, transparent gallery stands at the top, reproducing the peristyle of the Parthenon in terms of both orientation and size. The large open courtyard was conceived to accommodate the marbles and sculptures from the Acropolis. Careful lighting design has allowed the museum to be constructed on the basis of the collection of statues it will house.

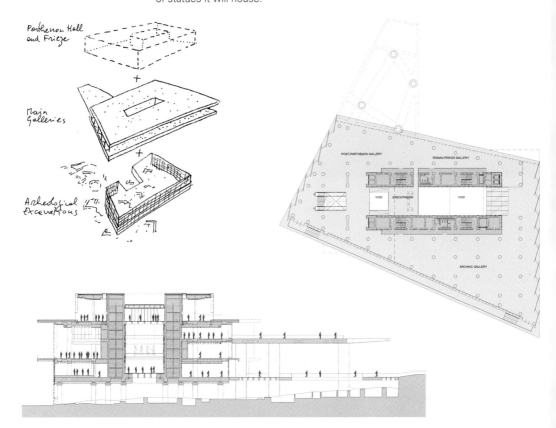

Rafael Moneo

Museum of the Roman Theatre

2007
Cartagena, Spain

An extensive archaeological area in Cartagena, Spain has been brought back to life with the discovery of an extraordinary 1st century BCE Roman theatre. The project seeks to connect the various topographical levels of the city. An incision is made in the nineteenth-century enclosure and the new structure is incorporated as a penetrating element that connects, underground below the roadway, to the Palacio Pascual de Riquelme, where the entrance to the museum is located. Then, from this new implant, a small passageway runs through the half shadows below the cathedral and gives access to the Roman Theatre. The archaeological experience is translated into a broader idea, seeking to connect the different historical periods represented by the succession of strata accumulating over the centuries. The museum represents both a passageway and a threshold between times, languages and cultures.

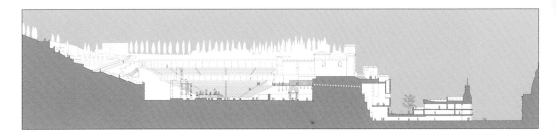

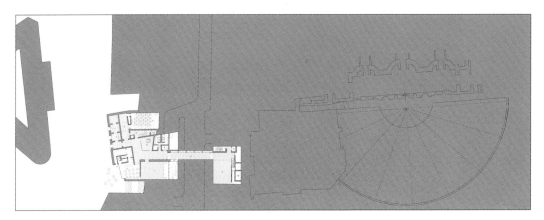

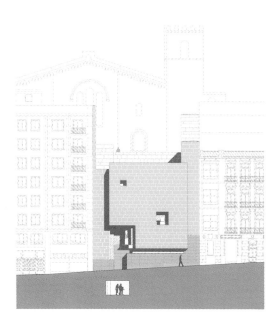

n!studio
Ferrini Stella Architetti
Associati

Breche and Noye Archaeological Museum and Research Centre

2006
Froissy, France

Located between two country roads, the museum establishes a rapport with the archaeological area behind it. It represents an excavation process, where the uplifted ground leaves a cavity that accommodates the exhibition facilities. This transformation of the land creates access, via a ramp in COR-TEN steel, to a way from the upper level of the site to the lower where the museum entrance is. The museum is conceived as a continuous passageway allowing visitors to cross through it from the outside to the inside. The exhibition area is located at the summit, with openings allowing natural light to penetrate. The offices and storage areas are located to the rear and illuminated via a zenith lighting system using skylights. The new project transforms into a platform, a natural substrate. The archaeological museum reinterprets the themes of primitive architecture, dug into the rock.

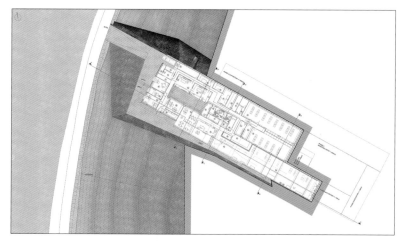

*n!*studio
Ferrini Stella Architetti
Associati

Museo Archeologico di San Vincenzo al Volturno

2006
Castel San Vincenzo,
Italy

This is a stratigraphic project composed of various materials—transparent, opaque, reflective. The plan comprises a gallery wrapped around an inner nucleus. The museum spaces have been designed to house medieval relics from the nearby Abbey of San Vincenzo al Volturno. The wall translates into a showcase. Openings at floor level provide views of the landscape below. The characteristically reddish copper panels with which the museum is faced integrate the building into its context in an almost mimetic way. At the same time, the project creates a dialectical relation with the site, with the building both anchored to the ground and projecting into the void. The volume exhibits a vocation for compactness, while its floor plan is prevalently characterized by the variety of its spaces arranged around the galleries. This interference between the simplicity of the external volume and the dynamism of the interior make the museum particularly attractive.

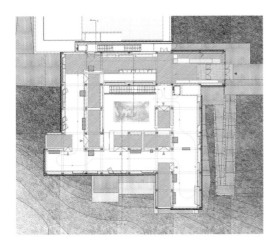
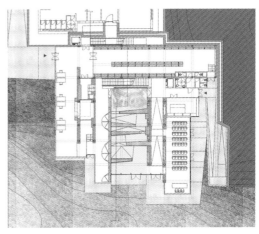

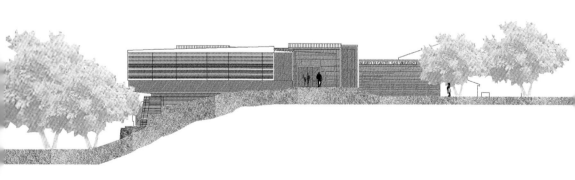

Dieguez Fridman
Associated Architects

Jeongok Prehistory Museum

2006
Gyeonggi-do,
South Korea

Archaeological findings unearthed in 1978 in the province of Gyeonggi-do, South Korea, dating to the Palaeolithic era provided the incentive behind the design competition for a Prehistory Museum organized by the municipality. The winning project seeks to resolve the relationship between nature and architecture, standing as an entry to the archaeological excavations. The body of the museum detaches from the ground to follow the contours of the local topography. Visitors descend from above into the exhibition halls, following a path leading to an underground space within the mountain. Viewed from below, the museum emerges in a form projected into the void, highlighting its implantation in the ground. The museum exhibits a technological and informatic vocation, offering not only information on the nature of the prehistoric findings but also achieving a formal and spatial harmony. Its shape is dictated by the principle of continuity, where volumes, openings for illumination, artificial spaces and natural settings lose their respective oppositions and merge into a new dialogue.

site plan
scale 1:1200

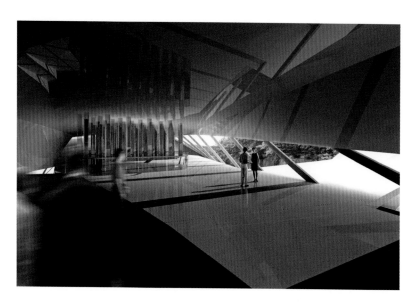

Jeongok Prehistory Museum

2006
Gyeonggi-do,
South Korea

The request for designs issued by the Gyeonggi Provincial Government in 2006 focused on the construction of a new prehistory museum with exhibition spaces and facilities for storage, educational programmes and recreation. The winning design entails a cut in the ground and the creation of an artificial platform where large eroded and excavated openings allow light to penetrate into the exhibition areas. At the foot of the ridge, a curved basalt wall, 91 metres long and 10 metres high, the same material of which the mountain is composed, leads to the entrance: a subterranean space illuminated through openings cut into the platform. Hidden in the ground, the museum is invisible from above. The designs create a dialogue between an orthogonal plan and its counterpart that is underground and archaic. The museum's foundations are rooted in the ground and its abstraction and rigorous geometry stand counter to the orographical variations of the site.

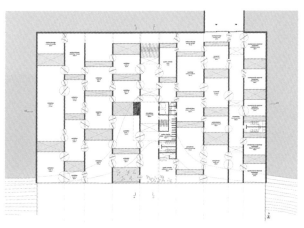

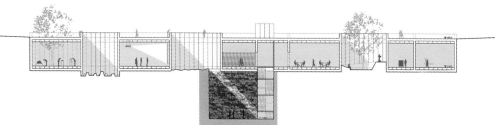

Gigon/Guyer Architekten
Annette Gigon,
Mike Guyer

Archaeological Museum and Park in Kalkriese

2002
Kalkriese, Germany

The Kalkriese museum and archaeological park are incorporated into a broad landscape marking the site of the Battle of the Teutoburg Forest, which took place in 9 CE. The building and park work together to create a setting where the Roman roads and the dense network of German trails are highlighted. Three multimedia pavilions denominated *seeing*, *hearing* and *understanding* are located in various positions in the park and offer a historical reconstruction of the site that the intervention defends and preserves. The archaeological area is enclosed in a fence of metal panels. The museum is a simple parallelepiped raised above the ground and surmounted by a belvedere-watchtower that affords a view of the entire plain. It has a forthright metal frame faced in COR-TEN steel panels. Within the archaeological theme of ancient traces brought back to life, the museum exhibits its transitory qualities and states its role as a workshop and laboratory seeking to accommodate and enhance the suggestive elements and nature of the site.

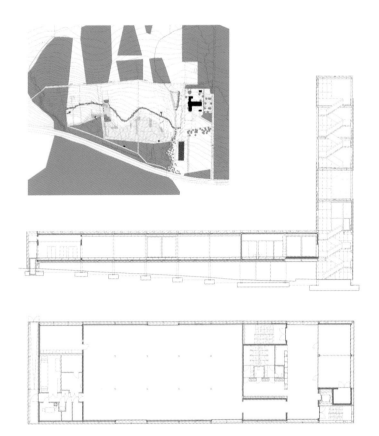

Implant

Cities, like history, are a collection of experiences that have accumulated like sediments over the centuries. Memory is a complex quantity of information that has been added up, erased, dispersed, or converted. Like existence itself, these dimensions of integration, completion or fragmentation lead us into a complex space. Entering into a time-honoured, life-worn body and implanting new vitality and new functions is a process that has witnessed different methods of application through time, methods deriving from the need to convert components of the environmental fabric that were originally developed for specific purposes. In the past, this process was a question of necessity and the transformation paid no heed to the document it was rewriting. In the current perspective, which is the product of decades of consolidated theory and practice of restoration, we acknowledge the deep-seated character of the monument that will undergo redevelopment. The purpose of the implantation of present time into a past context is to keep the old building alive and put it back into the service of the greater community. As a consequence, the museum that is born out of the transformation of a historical or industrial building can only be the result of a dedicated, surgical operation, given that the old structure is endowed with its own distinct character. And yet these are the projects that now offer the greatest potentials, in that they give back life to structures otherwise doomed to extinction. Such places, endowed with the allure of a life lived, acquire a new identity, in some cases as a memory of themselves and the functions that they once performed, in others as a place in which the expressions of our times find opportunities for dialogue. For example, contemporary art finds an extraordinarily evocative dimension in these abandoned and converted sites. They become relational spaces and their historical walls transform into backdrops for a new mindscape. The past reveals a great generosity when the architect succeeds in respecting and comprehending the material with which he or she will work. Never before have these sites offered such opportunities for exploration and new experiments. The charm of the revitalized factory or the military installation that comes back to life in a civilian guise presents us with one certainty: history is still the field in which memory, like a phoenix, rises from its own ashes.

Brückner & Brückner

Art Depot – Museum im Kulturspeicher

2002
Würzburg, Germany

One of the most extraordinary grain depots on the Main, in Würzburg, is reborn in a new guise as a museum of art. The project contemplates the stonework of the old granary and adds at either end enclosed volumes in steel and glass with inclined surfaces in light grey and brown stone that complement the chromatic characteristics of the original materials and allow natural light to enter. The exhibition halls are laid out on three levels. The bulk of the transformation work was done inside the old walls. Open space extends through the entire structure with ramps and walkways providing access to the exhibition spaces. The façade on the port side is characterized by the addition of two volumes in steel and glass, housing the cafeteria, offices and library and surmounted by two panoramic terraces. The project has respected the urban and social identity of the old structure and the new implant opens the grain depot once again to the city.

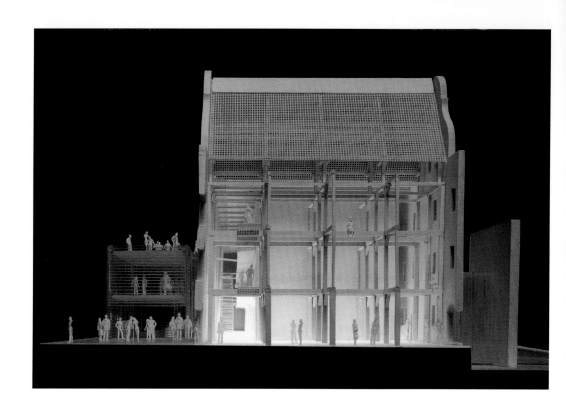

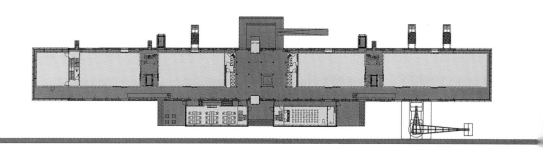

Herzog & de Meuron   **Tate Modern**

2000
Bankside, London, UK

The project regards the conversion of a former electrical power plant originally designed by Sir Giles Gilbert Scott in the period 1947-1963 and hence outfitted with strongly distinctive elements determining its identity: namely the brick smokestack and the turbine room. Located along the axis of Saint Paul's cathedral on the south bank of the Thames, the architects left its strongly characteristic exterior largely unmodified. Inside, the building was redeveloped using an essential language that respected the original layout. The façade, reminiscent of the Art Deco style, was preserved but surmounted by a two-storey structure in steel and glass, which creates a luminous connection while grafting on a simple and essential form. Access to the turbine hall, located below the level of the Thames, is provided by a broad ramp leading down to the lower altitude. This represents the principal inside modification. The enormous void space, accommodating modern and contemporary art, renders the new project one of the most interesting museums installed in a former industrial structure.

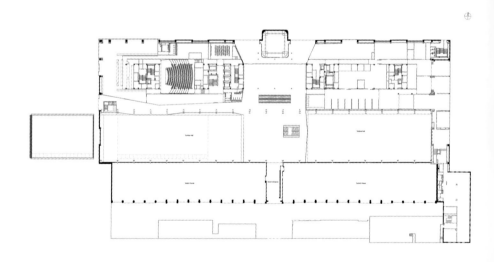

25m

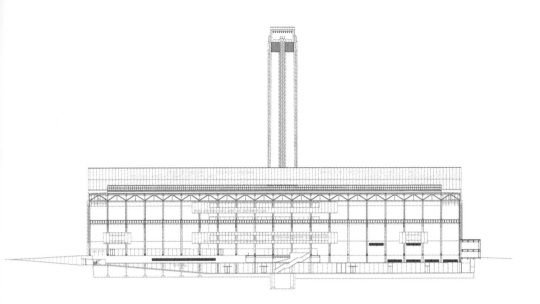

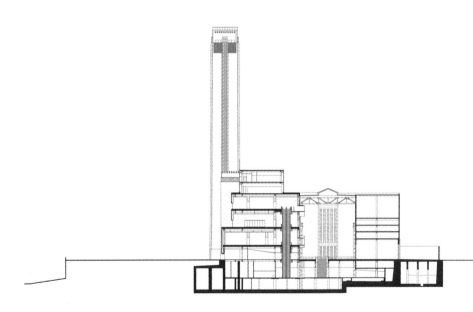

Michael Maltzan
Architecture

MoMA QNS

2002
Long Island City,
New York, USA

During the renovation work in the Manhattan MoMA, the institution was moved to Queens for three years. It took up residence in an abandoned factory in the industrial zone of Long Island City, which has now switched vocation to become a place for intercultural exchange. The project exalted the elementary characteristics of the factory's interior, creating a sense of tension between the spaces to reinforce the idea of movement. The new museum is characterized by unconfined exhibition spaces that favour programmatic interweaves and interactions. Externally, it preserves unaltered the industrial atmosphere and dimension in which it was generated and developed. A special wharf was built in Queens to receive the extraordinary collections from the Manhattan MoMA.

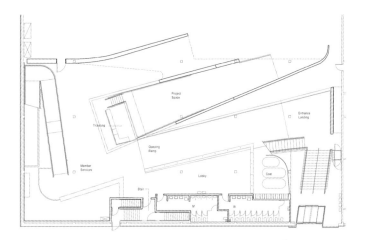

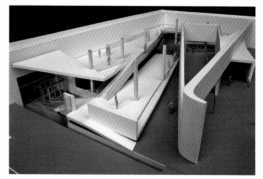

Nieto Sobejano
Arquitectos

San Telmo Museum Extension

2006
San Sebastián, Spain

The extension has been conceived as a green wall that establishes a new relationship with the historical building housing the Museum of San Telmo. Located between the edge of the city and Mount Urgull, it creates a new topographical environment. Two pavilions were designed to accommodate the facilities needed for the new programme of activities, thus including exhibition spaces, an auditorium, a multimedia centre, a cafeteria and educational facilities. As a sort of natural new surface, the extension brings the project to a state quite similar to its context as an interchange point between the city and the mountain behind it. The openings and entrances are ideated as excavations into the wall. A system of metal screens anchored to the wall provides places for plants, moss and lichens, which create a new surface and establish a special communion between the natural and the artificial. The architecture changes and evolves in a sort of organic process.

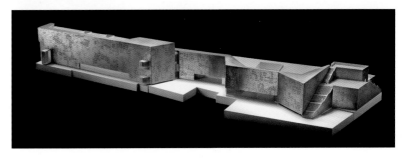

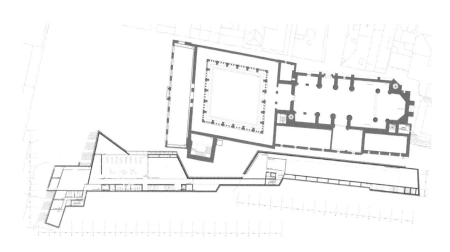

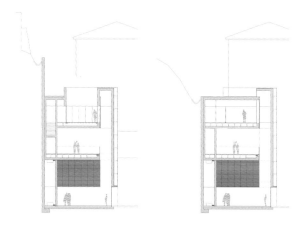

Nelson-Atkins Museum of Art

2007
Kansas City, Missouri,
USA

The need to extend the existing museum space, originally built in 1933, sparked an innovative thinking process resulting in five transparent elements radiating down a slope outward from the original building, all interconnected via underground passageways. The luminous showcases create a new relationship with the outdoor sculpture park. The museum transforms into a seeing machine, both from the outside in and vice versa, creating new perspectives and new relations with the pathways through the park. Light enters the new units through translucent glass to create natural suffused lighting. The new project demonstrates the architect's talent for using a compositional principle applied to different forms growing out of the local surroundings. Openings here and there reveal the internal ramps and the functional modes of these suggestive machines.

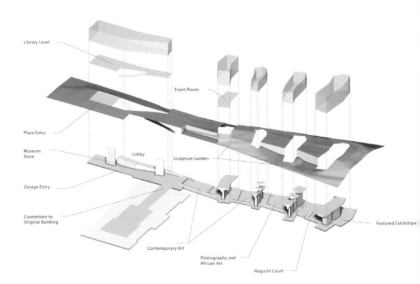

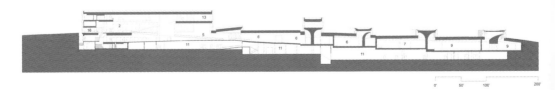

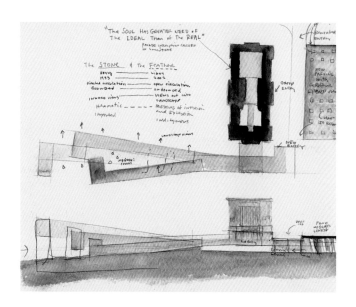

Pedro Barrié de la Maza Foundation

2005
Vigo, Spain

Created inside a building designed by Manuel Gómez Román and originally constructed in 1919, the headquarters of the Pedro Barrié Foundation exploits the potential offered by the structure and carves out broad open spaces to ensure both flexibility and functionality of use. Like a chamber of curiosities, the intervention has given material form to various functions. An air space was created behind the main façade, granting it room as if to show respect. The main activities are located in the internal unit, which accommodates the elevators giving access to the different levels. At the level of the entrance the lobby presents an extraordinary opportunity for transformation into a theatre thanks to technological installations. From this level, visitors gain access to the two upper exhibition halls, while the top level accommodates a conference room. Here, the seats can be lifted to allow diversified use of the space. This project is characterized as a merger between a museum and a theatre.

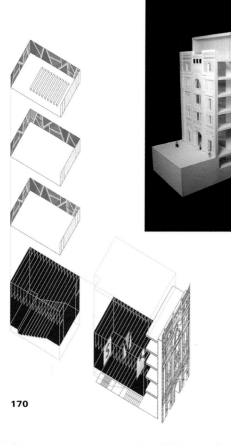

Cherubino Gambardella

Kunsthall at the *Mostra d'Oltremare* in Naples

2003
Naples, Italy

Damaged after the Second World War, the banking and trade pavilion built in 1938 by Bruno La Padula has been rebuilt and transformed into a Kunsthall. The project recovered all the remnants of the original plan. The decision to transform the building into a museum of contemporary art led to the choice of a rarefaction of information, both spatial and chromatic. The industrial concrete confers a uniform pattern while a system of ramps remakes the internal space into something of a promenade evoking rationalist design. In this revisitation and reinterpretation of modern architecture, the desire was to generate a place that moves in slow motion so as to offer maximum flexibility of use. Unlike redevelopment projects in industrial buildings, here the architects worked with void space.

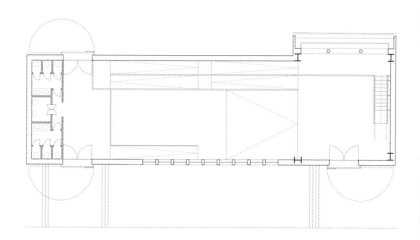

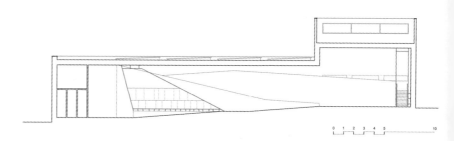

Studio Italo Rota
& Partners

Arengario Museo del Novecento

2002
Milan, Italy

Palazzo dell'Arengario, located in Milan's Piazza del Duomo, has been reconverted in the Museo del Novecento. It is a transformation that seeks to construct a simple circulation and exhibit system that will optimize the spaces, make the building a cultural hub and re-establish for it an eminent role in the city. A spiral ramp has been designed in the vertical space of the tower leading from the subway level up to the Sala delle Colonne and to the panoramic terrace overlooking Piazza Duomo. Within its dynamic volume, this futuristic machine translates into a system that both provides connections and becomes a venue for exhibitions. The ascent up the ramp leads to the room dedicated to the painter of *The Fourth Estate*, Giuseppe Pellizza da Volpedo. From here the visitor enters the rooms dedicated to movements from Futurism to Transavanguardia. The building will be completely restored and the walls faced in opaque glass panels to render the exhibitions independent of the original structure.

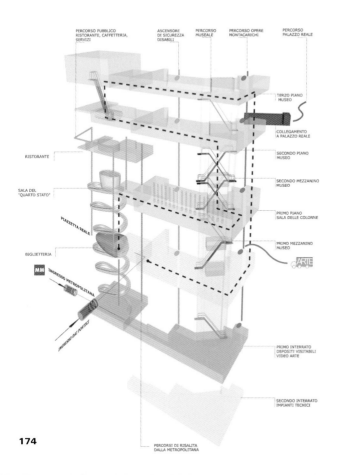

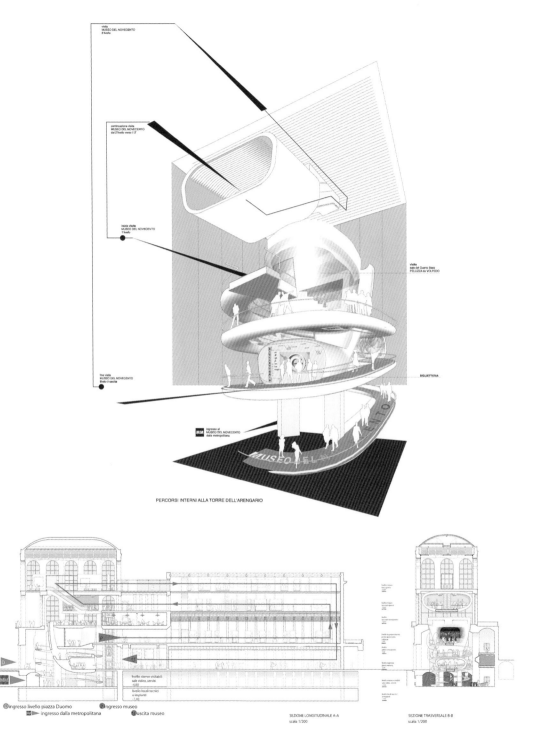

visita
MUSEO DEL NOVECENTO
3° livello

continuazione visita
MUSEO DEL NOVECENTO
dal 2°livello verso il 3°

inizio visita
MUSEO DEL NOVECENTO
1°livello

visita
sale del Quarto Stato
PELLIZZA da VOLPEDO

fine visita
MUSEO DEL NOVECENTO
livello 0 uscita

BIGLIETTERIA

MM ingresso al
MUSEO DEL NOVECENTO
dalla metropolitana

PERCORSI INTERNI ALLA TORRE DELL'ARENGARIO

livello riserve visitabili
sale video, servizi
-4,60

livello locali tecnici
e impianti

D ingresso livello piazza Duomo   **E** ingresso museo   **U** uscita museo
MM ingresso dalla metropolitana

SEZIONE LONGITUDINALE A-A
scala 1/200

SEZIONE TRASVERSALE B-B
scala 1/200

175

Wadsworth Atheneum Museum

2000
Hartford, Connecticut,
USA

The Wadsworth Atheneum is the oldest public art museum in the United States. It has undergone various expansions from 1842 to 1969 and now takes the form of five buildings that create a sort of campus. The extension project links the different buildings in order to improve both flows and internal connections. The new design involves a suspended and perforated metallic structure creating an internal court with transparent access. Positioned over this central area, the addition creates an elliptical movement that encounters the different levels of the pre-existing buildings. The new fluid and dynamic organism interlaces and joins the rigid grids of these volumes. A conical section allows natural light to penetrate down to the entrance level and marks the limit of the upward path.

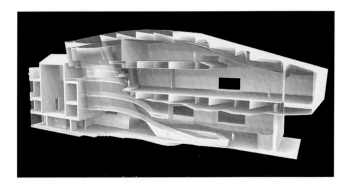

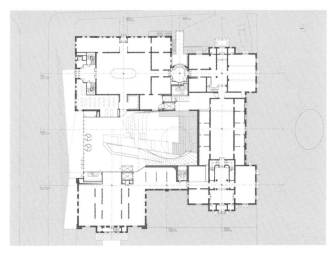

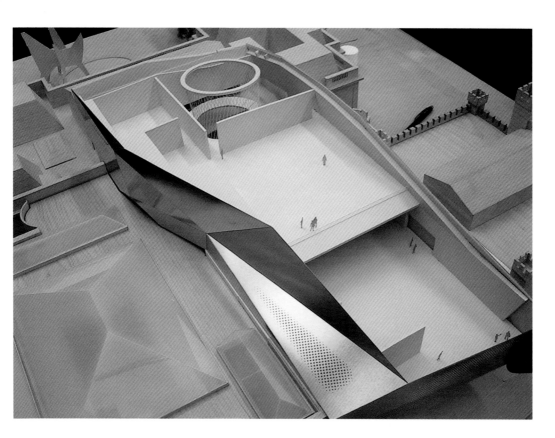

Daniel Libeskind   **Danish Jewish Museum**

2004
Copenhagen, Denmark

Within the orderly confines of the old section of the Royal Library of Copenhagen, the new museum, with its birch plywood panelling reminiscent of the boats that carried the Jews to safety, enters into contact and conflict with the brick walls of the historical structure.

The narration of the space and the materials follows historical experience, as a memory of the voyage in fishing boats across the sea to neutral Sweden by seven thousand Danish Jews in 1943 to escape Nazi persecution. A tight, transversal and autonomous dialogue is generated, but one which at the same time is confined and directed, and enriches the presence of the new. In crossing through these oblique spaces, illuminated by raking light, one has the sensation of making an unsteady voyage across the restless sea.

Nieto Sobejano
Arquitectos

Moritzburg Museum Extension

2009
Moritzburg, Germany

The project regards the expansion of the museum of art located since 1904 in the old castle of Moritzburg in Halle (Saale), a military structure built at the end of the 15th century. One of the goals was to get beyond the romantic image of the ruin that the monument communicates. The castle is a historical document that preserves its characteristic elements: the outer walls, three of the original four corner turrets, and the internal courtyard. The project entails the creation of a cover over the space, a folded platform whose dynamic configuration opens to let in the natural light. The new roof is made of aluminium, a material that clearly distinguishes itself from its archaeological counterparts. A new tower, 25 metres high, provides vertical access to the new galleries. The contemporary enters the old and generates a new inner landscape.

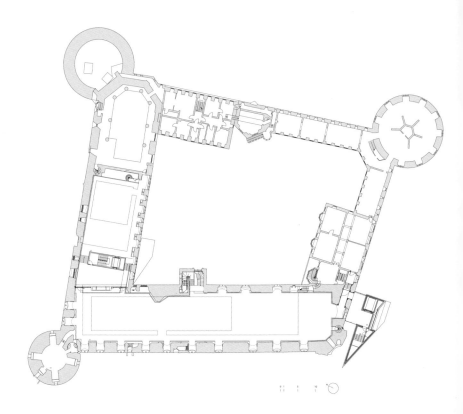

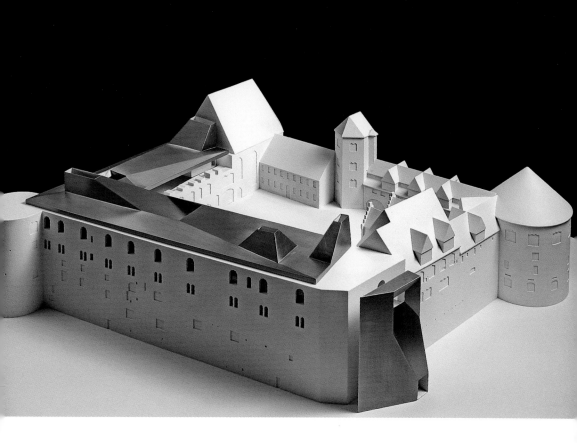

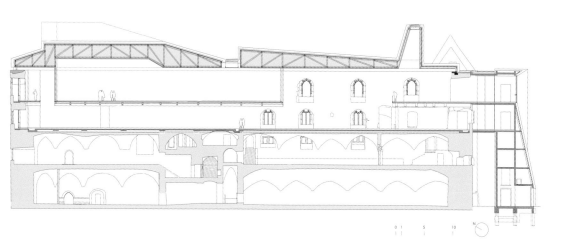

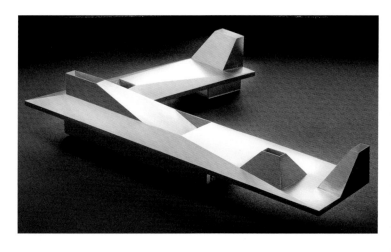

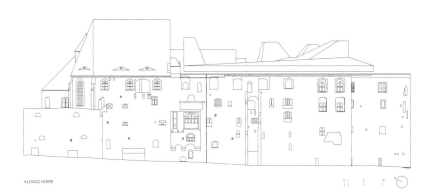

ALZADO NORTE

Markus Scherer
Walter Angonese
Klaus Hellweger

Restoration and museographic design for Castel Tirolo

2003
Tirolo, Italy

The restoration and museographic project for the Castel Tirolo historical museum involves the entire castle, including the fortified hill to the south, in regard for the principle that the museum draws its sustenance from the historical and material substance of the monument to safeguard and also from the qualities of the surrounding landscape. Following the fortified passage and passing through the refectory, one arrives in the keep, which has witnessed the greatest transformation in becoming a museum. Inside, a stairway comprising twenty-two landings is anchored to and wraps around a square steel pillar system that gradually widens upwards following the contours of the tapering walls. The progressive downward narrowing enhances the vertiginous sensation of the void as one climbs. The exhibits are set up on the landings, which are detached from the old walls of the keep, while the multimedia stations are positioned in the central balconies. Wood and COR-TEN steel are used as building materials to create an interesting intermingling of old and new. Their essential qualities generate a feeling of authenticity in the museum.

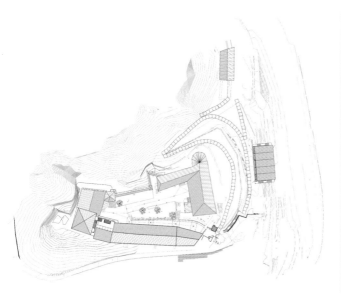

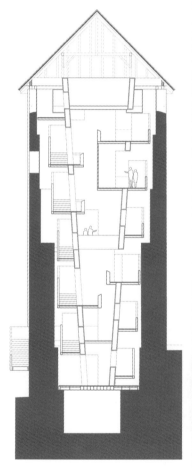

Meyer, Scherer
& Rockcastle

Mill City Museum

2004
Minneapolis, Minnesota,
USA

A museum of local history was created in Minneapolis inside the remains of an old grain mill built in 1880 and heavily damaged by fire in 1991. The new institution celebrates the historical industrial structure powered by the waters of the Mississippi. The mill, much of which was lost, has been rebuilt and redeveloped. A transparent structure, engaged in dialogue with the remnants of the old perimeter walls, marks the outlines of the project and constitutes a spectacular fore-space between the ruins and the new. Inside, the new spaces are integrated into the original iron framework, intermingling the functions and relations between industrial archaeology and contemporary architecture. These are perfect settings for re-evoking the age-old rites of material culture. Externally, the project restores dignity to this time-worn urban element celebrated as one of the city's monuments in 1980, one century after its birth, and which now, regarbed, lives again.

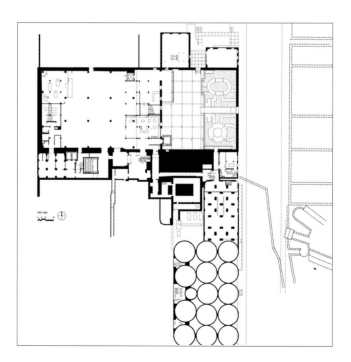

LIN Finn Geipel
+ Giulia Andi
Architects Urbanists

Alvéole 14 – Transformation of a submarine base

2007
Saint-Nazaire, France

This project involves the transformation of the submarine base at Saint-Nazaire, a city located on the Atlantic coast of France in the Pays de la Loire region, south of Brittany. The base was built in 1941-1943 by the German navy. A disquieting site of massive dimensions, 295 metres long by 130 metres deep, the new project seeks to transform and give new meaning to the spaces. Partially renovated, the complex now accommodates spaces for art (the first 14 pens giving onto the harbour) and contemporary music (inside the bunker). A carpet of lights marks out the inner walkways and the renovated spaces. Located at the mouth of the Loire River, the redeveloped complex offers a message of hope to a city for which the 'monument' has always represented the negative signs of its past. Here, military architecture is reborn as a civilian project.

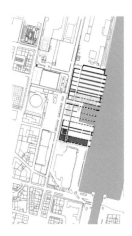

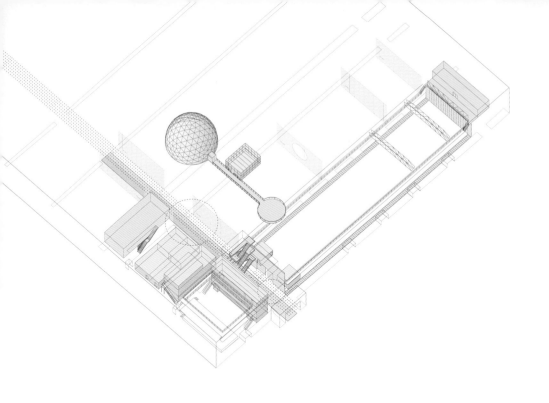

Inclusions: the museum as completion and transformation

When we address the issue of transforming a historical or industrial building, we are led to inquire into the temporal, cultural and stylistic dimensions that have preceded us. We often feel a sort of reverence toward the past, attributing a profound dignity to its monuments. We are somewhat in awe of the places where our forebears left their tracks, whether they are enduring and tangible marks or ephemeral traces.

This encounter or dialogue has witnessed different interpretations and significant changes over the centuries. In the Middle Ages, materials were recovered from previous structures and, valued exclusively in terms of their technical and structural qualities, used in new buildings to create a collage of new compositions. The Renaissance witnessed a renewed quest for Classical proportions based on observations of the original ancient Roman architecture. 19th-century theorists saw the past as a living material. The principles of *stylistic restoration* elaborated by Eugène Viollet-le-Duc stated that the monument can be transformed. His desire to safeguard and conserve ancient and historic buildings led him to dictate new plans using new linguistic conquests in a phase characterized by an eclectic style. His work ensured the continued existence of many medieval complexes, but critics saw in his heavy alterations an often overambitious attitude, bringing about radical transformations of the historical document upon which he made his 'inscriptions.' John Ruskin took an opposite view. He felt that because of the significant alterations it caused, restoration was the principal cause for the loss of authenticity in a work. He proposed an aesthetics of the ruins, taken to the extreme of advocating the natural death of a historical factory.

The dialogue with and reinterpretation of the past are still tainted with a sort of original sin and collide or clash with the theories aimed at the historical and philological conservation of monuments. The unresolved theoretical issue regards works which by their nature have been built as units composed of hierarchically consequential parts and the transformation of these works.

Entering a historical building and transforming it implies for the architect a realignment with the present time. Hence originated the philosophy of working *between* the elements, with tesserae that are inserted in the spaces formed within the weave or grid that has embodied the life of the historical document. This is a way that museography encounters the theme of lacunae, voids, missing parts, and thus a broader idea of restoration work. Carlo Scarpa was unquestionably an architect who introduced a new way of approaching the transformation of a unitary architectural organism. His Museum of Castelvecchio involved an intervention on a medieval castle in Verona (1354–56) built by Cangrande II della Scala. In the period from 1956 to 1964, after innumerable revisions, Scarpa gave it a new life, setting it up as a worksite where the contemporary age and history are creating a new composition based on getting beyond a coherent, analogous image that had been crushed by the past. He worked within an existing situation, he excavated material, incorporated tesserae, looking at the space with the help of the perspective of a moving spectator or subject.

Leaving the axonometric view behind, something which had been an integral part of the modernist architectural interpretation, the Venetian architect gives birth to a new interpretation based on graftings. He parted ways with the idea of thinking of the past as a frozen space and created strongly characterized places where, by means of inclusions, ancient and present space fuse together. He used rough materials such as unfinished cement and a construction technique placing care on the arrangement of the wood used to build the formworks, and also noble and precious materials, such as brass and rosewood. The work was marked by an extraordinary attention to detail. Scarpa generated a new philosophy of developing museums in historical buildings.

Today the need to reintegrate these settings, these urban bodies, into the contemporary era is a priority. And there is also the need to give back life and meaning to these structures, which originated with different purposes and ends. The debate on what to do with ancient or historical buildings or archaeological fragments was given a new and strong impetus in the mid-1980s by two Spanish projects: Giorgio Grassi's reconstruction of the Roman theatre in Sagunt and Rafael Moneo's museum in the city of Merida. These fall into the category of interventions in historical memory that penetrate into the organism, conditioning it and forcing it to assume a new identity.

In the early decades of the twentieth century, the German architect Heinrich Tessenow pondered the character of buildings, proposing an idea of construction based on simplicity and objective clarity as a reflection of an inner order.

The integration of a museum into a pre-existing structure has always marked a moment of critical review. It means making choices regarding a text that is already written, adding or removing words, with all the problematics that such decisions may bring.

In 1985, during a period when Post-modernism was proposing citationist imitations of items of the past, Moneo designed the Museum of Roman Art in the small Spanish city of Merida. It was conceived as a showcase embracing within it the local archaeological area. He reinterpreted both the spatial and the structural principles of Roman architecture, adding in elements of the tectonic conception of structure theorized by Louis Kahn years before. Moneo focused on the section in his work. The material, comprising mortarless brick walls, represents an abstract landscape, in which the melancholy of the round arches coexists with metaphysical landscapes à la de Chirico, evoking Roman spaces in a mixture of myth and modernity.

One enters this conflictual place and finds surfaces and masses that have recorded both ancient history and that of the 20th century; one finds overlaid the architectures of ancient Rome, Piranesi, Behrens and Kahn. Moneo came up with a new reading of this site with its sedimented strata, but the rules guiding the project still felt the influence of the city formulated by Aldo Rossi, which adhered to the ordering principle of the road. Indeed, the layout is informed by the geometry of the circulatory system of the modern city, while inside the archaeological area it is rotated along the axes of the original foundation.

If we extend our analysis, looking through a magnifying glass or taking a satellite perspective, we realize that the city has always operated on itself in a sort of museographic process. It is a living and stratified body, a place of renewal, rising from its own rubble, a scenic space in continual evolution, in which the new incorporates itself into the weave of the old.

Paris, Berlin and Frankfurt are the cities that have generated the bulk of the literature in this regard. The urban plans of Georges Eugène Haussmann in the French capital, ordered by Napoleon III, introduced a method of operating on the urban body similar to that of a surgeon. Think of the transformation that the city, with its medieval layout, experienced in the period of 1853–70, with the opening of broad boulevards to replace neighbourhoods deemed unwholesome. Work was undertaken in the historic city to modernize the sewer system and to incorporate new public spaces and works that responded to the needs and characteristics of a new society. The city declared itself to be an open-air museum, whose contents were renewable.

Over a century later, after the revolution in consumption patterns and consumer goods, the intervention that strongly suggested the idea of a graft was that championed by the then President François Mitterand at the Louvre in 1989. In the central courtyard, the architect Ieoh Ming Pei created a large glass pyramid, the entrance to the Louvre's new underground expansion, which doubled the exhibition space of the historical museum and introduced services and functions to meet the needs of an increasingly heterogeneous public, mirroring the complex functions of the city within the space of the museum.

Berlin and Frankfurt are somewhat different texts in that the bombardments of the Second World War wiped out entire zones of the city, including the most significant public areas. This tragic destiny dictated their rebirth in that the redefinition of their lost outlines became a necessity. While Berlin has represented the grandest contemporary urban worksite, it is on the banks of the Main, in the heart of a Frankfurt devastated by the War, that a system of museums was created with the goal of establishing an ideal reconstruction of the city through a project of memory.

The design competition for the Dom-Römerberg district in Frankfurt in the mid-1980s was an occasion for inquiring into the theme of architectural design in terms of memory, renewal and contemporary design and offers insights into the museum-city relationship. In the eyes of the jury, composed of Ungers and Böhm, the Schirn Kunsthalle in Römerberg (1980–86), designed by Bangert, Jansen, Scholz and Schultes, reflected a monumental urban plan which, in the portico connecting the cathedral with the city hall, evoked the role of the connecting elements within the urban tissue represented by the cruciform layouts of the 19th-century arcades. In this view, the museum certainly looked to the city to unite the grid-like fabric of dwellings rebuilt in keeping with history and, at the same time, generate new urban loci, avoiding direct stylistic spin-offs of the monumental buildings already present within the context.

In 1990, Pippo Ciorra wrote an essay titled *Dalla città-museo al museo-città* [*From the city-museum to the museum-city*], recording an interpretation of the museum project as a sort of urban system, a complex image of empty and occupied spaces, plazas and confines, that incorporated the mechanisms of the public space. In the 1980s and early 1990s, a vision of the museum was developed as a reflection of the image of the city.[1] It contains an interpretation of the museum project as a piece of a larger idea, as a part within a whole. The *urbs* has always been planned as a place of memory: its structure has been conceived to accommodate events and, in the flow of time and languages, ideated as an open-air museum.

The 1980s was a season in which architects looked carefully upon the museum-city model. In 1984 with his Neue Staatsgalerie in Stuttgart, James Stirling offered the project that perhaps best incarnated the principle of the museum as an urban system. It is a complex and varied container engaged in dialogue with the Neoclassical building standing opposite. Its central courtyard acts as an interchange node for this multi-stratified document, a passage between inside and outside, between history and the city as a broader reference system.

In Berlin, Aldo Rossi proposed the Deutsches Historisches Museum (1987). While remaining on paper, it is perhaps one of the most exhaustive projects of his production. It was a project that contained within it, like a collage of the ideal city, residential units, the Renaissance rotunda that functioned as a connector among the parts, and the colonnade that allowed interrelations between the museum spaces and their urban counterparts. The Milanese architect had brought together into a single system all the complexity of a piece of the city both historical and modern.

In the Wexner Center for the Arts (1983–89) in Columbus, Peter Eisenman characterized the front with the urban theme of towers commemorating the history of the site. At the same time, as pointed out by Antonino Saggio, in the three-dimensional structure of the frame, grafted on between pre-existing structures, he broke up the symmetrical and self-referential schemas of the nostalgic Post-modern languages and opened the way to an idea of deconstruction.[2]

The generation that made its main mark in the 1980s thought above all to interact with and conserve the image of the city itself. The trend in Milan and the studies by Aldo Rossi had incorporated the urban rules of the ancient city back into architecture and rendered clear and evident the monument's aspiration to endure through time.

Toward the close of the decade, Hans Hollein offered one of the most suggestive designs (unfortunately never built) in the Museum in the Mönchsberg, which would have been dug into the famous cliff overlooking Salzburg and been built almost completely without a need for exterior walls. With this project the Austrian architect opened the way to the theme of excavation in the grand basin leading to the subterranean spaces and that represented an inverse reference to Frank Lloyd Wright's Guggenheim. The interlacing paths, offering the possibility to visit the exhibition rooms according to whim, referred to the idea of an experiential museum as theorized by the American psychologist and pedagogue John Dewey. But most significantly, this project annulled the idea of the museum as a projection of the city.

In 1988, the *Deconstructivist Architecture* exhibition at the MoMA in New York, curated by Philip Johnson and Mark Wigley, gave momentum to new dynamics of composition at a time when the crisis in the real estate market had intellectuals, promoters and artists wondering about the sense of architecture. It was no longer the image of the historical city to dictate the rules; new places, interstitial spaces, the philosophy of *between* were what prevailed. This season's players were Eisenman, Gehry, Hadid, Coop Himmelb(l)au, Koolhaas, Tschumi and Libeskind. The exhibition would change orientations. It was no longer the history of the enclosed and self-referential document that would establish the confines of the composition, nor the consequential and hierarchical idea associated with the lexical and urban structure. The city is vivisected, memory is severed and uprooted.

In the 1980s, in a battle against the ideas of the Modern Movement, memory was reassigned to the orderly spaces of classicism, while deconstruction re-examined the most powerful figures in the early years of the 20th century: Boccioni, Balla, Duchamp, Melnikov, Tatlin, El Lissitzkij, Terragni, Le Corbusier, and Mies van der Rohe. The disruptive force of the futurist, constructivist and suprematist current in Russia resurfaced in the identity of this current, but also that of the heroic figures of the Modern Movement: Gropius' Bauhaus, Terragni of the Sant'Elia Kindergarten, the expressionist Le Corbusier of Ronchamp, and the transparency of Mies van der Rohe in the Farnsworth House.

This change of course is fundamental in interpreting the museum of the 1990s. The shift was made from the museum-city to the museum-graft. The themes addressed in these years regarded the need to intervene in areas that are marginal or residual, replacements or additions. The opportunities were represented by areas that had an abstract figuration. Works were not built in empty spaces via the typical introduction of an enclosed geometrical figure, but as tesserae inserted into a weave that was often already destructuralized in terms of form. Some critics have theorized that part of the deconstructivist movement developed thanks to the projects in residual spaces, which forced architectural composition to break with certain aprioristic structures.

This attitude, which is not dictated exclusively by a linguistic choice, brought the culture of the time to address the idea of the museum as an interrelational space, a *between* space, as an inclusion between unitary organisms. The shift in method came about for two principal reasons: the decentralization of the works and the recovery of pre-existing buildings.

When museum projects move away from the historical centre into the suburbs or periphery, the principles of seeking a dialogue with history no longer find an amenable or corresponding fabric in the discontinuous and incoherent nature of the outskirts.

The location naturally affects the design choices. The museum is not merely a container for art, it is itself a subject in space.

The 1990s witnessed a crisis in the theoretical model still centred on a structural approach to the relation between the building and its generative path. Today the trend in museums is to recover industrial areas, abandoned sites, brownfields, and to preserve them, give them back an identity and a dignity. These areas adjacent to the historical centre or the peripheral areas have offered architectural culture its greatest opportunities for exploration and inquiry via the process of conversion.

What are the potentials of these projects?

There are many reasons behind the choice of these structures. These old factories have a beauty in their weathered materials and often a melancholy charm in their quality of having experienced 'life.' The museum becomes a sort of Foucaultian heterotopia, i.e., it represents a multilayered site bearing a host of interconnected memories. Industrial archaeology offers less resistance than its ancient counterpart and the transformations can be more incisive.

These places are the ones that currently are best suited to act as venues for contemporary art, given the shift from the idea of finished work to that of a process that takes form in its interaction with the site, as in site-specific projects. In a sort of Duchampian revelation, art becomes charged with environmental relations. In this process, work, space and material are not disjoint but interpenetrating, inter-referencing, and take on new meanings. As a consequence, the work no longer has an absolute value, as once informed the museological quest in the 1920s and 1930s. Duchamp moved art into a mental space, into a game of chess.

The traditional museum model began to be questioned starting in the 1960s. In 1966, Robert Venturi theorized in his book *Complexity and Contradiction in Architecture* that architecture itself was modified in terms of its underlying principles by the inclusion of other memories that derived from the world of market goods, cinema and television.[3]

In 1968, when social transformations that were pushed further by art had led to new views of the world, the Institutional Critique movement was born, formed by the artists Marcel Broodthaers, Daniel Buren, Michael Asher and Hans Haacke with the aim of contrasting, via a critical process, museums that were no longer capable of accommodating new artistic expression.

This period was characterized by a schism between society and its institutions generated by deep upheavals in the world order. We will review a number of spheres, from art to cinema, that generated a new interpretation of the relation between body and graft to get a better understanding of the relationship between memory and inclusion.

In her essay *Reinventing the Medium*, where she speaks of action painting and the drip technique developed by Jackson Pollock in the late 1940s, Rosalind Krauss highlights a new way of conceiving the work of art. Pollock's technique involved dripping paint onto a canvas from a saturated paintbrush to create informal landscapes. The crucial shift was in moving the artistic process from a vertical plane to a horizontal position. Bereft of the usual support, this art, according to Krauss's thinking, threw easel painting into crisis. With this change in the work, which from now on would enter the realm of installations, the space became the new support for contemporary art.[4]

With Pop Art, the civilization of expression sought to get beyond the artist-work bond through the use of materials obtained from objects commonly used in consumer culture, transforming advertising images into icons. This inclusive category certainly embraced artistic pursuits ranging from Kurt Schwitters with his *Merzbau* (1920–36) and his art of found objects to the mid-1960s works of Jasper Johns, in which mass culture encountered the accumulation of polysemous materials, a metaphor of the waste of overproduction dictated by unnecessary rules.

It was a phase in history when time was marked by a strong acceleration as well as by a deep crisis in the international scenario. Let us review a few historical dates: in 1961, Yuri Gagarin was the first man to travel in space while the Berlin Wall, which would become the symbol of the Cold War, was being built; in 1962 the Vietnam War began; in 1963 President John F. Kennedy was assassinated. This transformation of the world, which was also influenced by the introduction of the birth control pill and its effect on sexual relations, with a new image associated with pleasure, culminated in 1969 with Neil Armstrong's walk on the moon. This mission marked a new vantage point on the world, now viewed from the moon.

Our perception of the body changed, both in art and in philosophy, and as a consequence our ability to relate to life-worn bodies, such as industrial facilities, where it was now possible to confer new life. Let us take a brief look at a number of crucial shifts.

The twilight of the museum-organ view in favour of the prosthetic view was anticipated in philosophy. The former reflected the objective ideals of Modernity, in the one-to-one relation between form and function, still in a clinical sense, while the latter, analyzed in Post-structuralist philosophy, grew out of a battle against the idea of hierarchical space dictated by static functions.

In 1972, Gilles Deleuze and Felix Guattari addressed the theme of the *body without organs* in their book *Anti-Œdipus*, in which they interpreted the individual as a *desiring machine*. The subject analyzed by the philosophers is incoherent, irreconcilable, schizophrenic and deterritorialized. Desire had supplanted the needs by which Freudian psychoanalysis established the rules of a conventionally understood being in the modern era. The body without organs highlights the thinking about the subject in the absence of rules, hierarchies or aprioristic constructs.[5]

Several years later, cinema and science fiction turned to the construction of artificial intelligence: androids and cyborgs, man-machine hybrids, nature and artifice. The human body had absorbed into itself the technological prostheses. Cinematography began to predict, toward the end of the 1970s, the insertion, as in the medical field, of extraneous bodies into abdomens, from video cassettes to alien beings, examples being Ridley Scott's *Alien* (1979) and David Cronenberg's *Videodrome* (1983). In this view, the body becomes vulnerable to these inner parasites.

This inclusive interpretation shifts from the lines internal to the individual to the solid ones of museum architecture by means of an interference, a virus, that has infected and liquefied its very substance. The visions demonstrated an analogy between the human body and that of the city, as part of the same substance, now inexorably mutant.

Hence the museum now incorporates other structures, other machines. The idea of penetrating into the places of the past, like a parasite that modifies the memory of them from within, took form around the mid-1990s. But it was conceptual art, installing itself in spaces that had already been lived in or that were characterized by the marks of war, that decreed, many years earlier, a new aesthetic.

Today the industrial areas, the old factories, the slaughterhouses, the prisons, the ruins of 17th-century structures or contaminated lands are transformed via minimal interventions into incredible mnemonic machines. But this is not constructed, it is already given. The space and the work establish a new symbiosis or a dialectical clash. These places meet the needs of the artists who communicate new relations to the observer.

At the same time, the paradox of our time is perpetuated, in which thousands of things remind us that we belong to the world of information travelling at the speed of light in a network in which we are all wrapped, in the final analysis actors in a story that no longer seems to belong to us.

Within the loss of memory, in an oblivion that is necessary for the construction of new syntaxes, these places claim a profound authenticity. They are real in that they have witnessed life, they have been coloured by the infinite defeats and victories to which history has subjected them.

Joseph Beuys was the first artist to grasp the need to shift the sense of place. It could no longer be a container meant to preserve a memory. There is no longer any showcase capable of gathering shared sentiments. Art encounters the site and its specificity. These are the experiences of a new way of experiencing the present within a characterized space, that conserves its own identity within it. Over time, out of this grew a philosophy of redevelopment of abandoned or former industrial sites that had formerly, in a previous life, served other purposes. These settings have a regressed memory, where one breathes the aura of the life-worn, where the space that is being consumed remembers, in the dismembered body, that it has a multiple nature. Within these spaces the artist operates with nothingness: all that is necessary is to bring in scraps and wastes to explain the meaning of his or her work.

Conceptual art introduced us into a specific and authentic dimension of space, where the museum is an environment, an open space, manifold experience, meanings that cause new questions to spring forth. In the final analysis, Beuys had grasped that art exists in a dualism between memory and forgetfulness, as in his *Fat Chair* where a wedge of fat made it impossible to sit down, invoking a sensation that is as disagreeable as it is surreal. The idea came from the artist's experience during WWII as an aviator for the Nazis in the Luftwaffe after his plane was shot down over Crimea. He claims he was saved by his 'enemies' who covered him with fat and felt to keep him from dying of cold. Felt and fat represent in his work this necessary reconciliation with nature and society. Moreover, his material drives the observer into an environment of the mind, arousing instinctual memories.

The artist whose work heralded the idea of the inclusive museum is Gordon Matta-Clark. In his 1974 work *Splitting*, he sliced through a pre-existing structure. This cut in a very familiar structure, a house, invited the viewer to rethink the unity that had been violated, the empty space in which the contemporary age inserts its symbols. For the Paris Biennial in 1975, Matta-Clark created the work *Conical Intersect*, piercing two nearby buildings undergoing demolition in the area where the Pompidou Centre would be completed (1977). He emptied out a part of the urban text and left a disturbing cavity 4 metres wide running through the two anonymous buildings. Art thus reviews itself (the metaphor was clearly associated with the eye and its capacity to observe and discern) through the elimination of matter, an immersive excavation inside a mental void. Anti-monuments as anti-architecture is the current that Matta-Clark created to remind us that the things we build are always social projects. These were years in which art, engaged in an ideological and political battle, came out of the museums to occupy the media and the public spaces that had been wrested away from the powers of the time.

In the interventions into pre-existing structures, the museum, erstwhile temple of memory, became the complex frame for events, the actor on a stage that involves performances by other subjects as well. The grand productive machines—whether industrial facilities, military areas or archaeological remains—have predetermined genes, they have already lived a life. In the past, the museum was a machine that not only served but was also profoundly symbolic of national identity and power. Today, these places no longer represent the civil venue of a political institution as much as a space tormented by an identity that in many ways is multiple. Like an alien, one enters an experience that already has a life of its own. This intromission, this modification of the organism from within, is certainly a phenomenon that represents one of the most problematic and fascinating aspects of the new museum institutions.

We have witnessed in the past radical alterations of structures designed for specific functions. Such is the tormented story of the Teatro Marcello in Rome, converted into a fortress in the Middle Ages and then into a residence by Baldassarre Peruzzi in the 16th century. This leads us into a new paradigm, in which the typological body is no longer unitary. This identity thus also includes change, events, accidents, chance.

In 2000, the Herzog & de Meuron studio completed one of the most successful projects of transformation of an industrial structure, generating wide interest for this type of operation. It was the conversion of a former electrical power plant originally designed by Sir Giles Gilbert Scott in the period 1947–63 and hence outfitted with strongly distinctive elements determining its identity: namely the brick smokestack and the turbine room. Located along the axis of Saint Paul's Cathedral on the south bank of the Thames, the architects left its strongly characteristic exterior largely unmodified. Inside, the building was redeveloped using an essential language that respected the original layout. The façade, reminiscent of the Art Deco style, was preserved but surmounted by a two-storey structure in steel and glass, which creates a luminous connection while grafting on a simple and essential form. Access to the turbine hall, located below the level of the Thames, is provided by a broad ramp leading down to the lower level. This represents the principal modification to the interior space. The enormous void space, accommodating modern and contemporary art, renders the new project one of the most interesting museums installed in a former industrial structure.

Among the most interesting conversion projects, we may also mention the master plan for the Zollverein Industrial Complex in Essen by the OMA group (2001), where visitors follow the same route by which coal was produced, the Kulturspeicher in Würzburg by Brückner & Brückner (2002), who introduced polished surfaces to heighten the effect of the stonework of the old factory, the Mill City Museum in Minneapolis by Meyer, Scherer & Rockcastle (2004), a transparent machine situated between the burnt-out walls of a factory, and the extreme project for the Transformation of a Submarine Base in Saint-Nazaire by the LIN group (2007), a cyclopean complex that symbolizes the futility of war. The U-boat pens, contaminated, life-worn, tragic containers, now provide exhibition space for contemporary works of art in keeping with the principle of interaction between the exhibition and its environmental setting.

These museums are antithetical to the 'neutral' ones of the Modern Movement's White Cube, where many memories are celebrated. Here, the neutral space highlighted the work under multicoloured lights, while in these new contexts it is the place that is loaded with pathos, of a time that has witnessed the material manifestation of an event that is spectacular or theatrical in itself. The industrial building, in which machines were reiteratively engaged in the serial production of Modernity, was a type that fascinated Walter Gropius. In 1911, he prepared for Karl Ernst Osthaus a series of photographs of the modern architecture. From this selection, emerged images of silos in the United States, which he saw as authentic and necessary structures, a spare beauty and the aspiration to a social principle. Over time, with the decommissioning of the factory, which had come to represent an existence, this structure took on the colours of a new immaterial substance. A short circuit was created and the spaces were decontextualized by the agency of the works they accommodated. These places construct a theatre of the world offering a setting that is already meaningful in its own right, as if a garment had been sewn over it.

In order to enter this dimension, which addresses the mental time of the present with the voice of the chronological time of the past, in the interpenetration of different structures, cultures and institutions, we may invoke the writings of Marcel Proust. In his *À la recherche du temps perdu*, on which he worked from 1906, following the death of his mother, with whom he had an almost morbid bond, until 1922, Proust described the story of a writer who seeks to reconstruct his life as a trace and to give meaning to his existence. The recovery of the past does not come about via *voluntary memory*, that which remembers events devoid of the emotions and sentiments that generated them, but by means of *involuntary memory*, which offers us, through an *interference of the heart* triggered by a sensation, a gesture or a taste, the images and perceptions of that which we have experienced. This recovered time comes back to life again, healed, as Debenedetti points out, redeemed from a malignant self-destructiveness. Clearly, this relation between the past and the present is a revision, a reconstruction of a dialogue of processes that are not only mental but also sensory. The memory lives again in virtue of a previous time. But art has shifted the field of observation from ocular vision to synesthetic sight, which brings the other senses into the interplay.

When the museum insinuates itself into the context of a sedimented memory, it can only be a search for what has been lost. As a consequence, in the tormented climate of recent years we are observing new phenomena that open the theme of the museum to interesting contaminations.

While in the past, knowledge was always seen as the purview of the few, the critic and man of letters Walter Benjamin had discerned, in 1936, in the technical ability to make reproductions in prints, photographs and especially in cinema, the possibility of rendering culture democratic and transmissible. Having overcome the dialectic of *hic et nunc*, of the here and now, which dictated the uniqueness of the traditional artistic act, fixed to a given time and place, the artistic process subsists as a medium, a filter between society and changes. In the moment, the precise instant, that our perception of the world is altered by art, our relationship to memory also changes. Think of the extraordinary transformation sparked by the camera. It seems to be a secondary thing, but with Nadar and the first cameras that recorded cities and landscapes, the artist was stripped of the magic of transforming reality by means of technique and content. The *camera obscura* shifted the vantage point on art, which inexorably, just a few decades after the introduction of photography and aroused by the horror of the impending war, would shift the interpretation of the world from the outside of the subject to the inside. This is the shift that we admiringly observe in the historical avant-garde movements and explicitly from currents ranging from expressionism through abstractionism.

But the darkness, this *camera obscura* of thought, led us into other settings. Plato's mythological cave once again became an imposing icon in reminding us of the origin of art as a projector of images. The philosopher stages a difficult scene, charged with symbolism, of people imprisoned right from birth, chained by their necks and forced to gaze upon a wall. Behind the prisoners there is a fire and between them a wall that represents a filter, a distance. People transporting objects or animals behind the prisoners cast their shadows on the wall, and the prisoners interpret these shadows as real things.

This separation between reality and its representation takes us into the theme of inclusive memory, into the interference between codes and cultures. In his text *A caverna: romance*, Saramago addressed the Platonic myth of images. He tells the tale of an old potter, Cipriano Algor, and the difficulty he had selling his wares in a hypertechnological context in which people were no longer interested in what he had to sell. 'The Centre,' a post-industrial institution, deemed that the potter's products were no longer useful. Cipriano proposed a new product and was forced to move inside, living and spending his time in the spaces of this infinite city-machine, like a baroque or Piranesian monster with tunnels, corridors, stairways, restaurants, a labyrinth of desires, the centre to all outskirts. The writer described the global world, devoid of specificity, where power and control exist together with the vacuity and futility of things.[6]

Saramago ventures into Orwellian literature and the films of Debord and writes about the final frontier where the virtual combines with the real and the potential replaces objective reality. Together with his son-in-law Marçal Gacho, who works in the Centre as a guard, the potter discovers the most powerful secret of the city-machine: the cave deep in its bowels. Saramago includes myth within the place of consumption, leaving the reader in a space of doubt, uncertainty, where even hope becomes a market commodity.

Out of this dimension emerge two fundamental *topoi* of inclusive memory: the museum as a place of commerce; and a new relation between art and entertainment. The idea of the museum as a frontier of hyper-consumerism was theorized a number of years ago by Franco Purini, who proposed an analogy between the places suited for communicating the new views of art and the shopping malls. It was a development toward the non-places conventionally used as the cathedrals of our times. The museum incorporates functions that belong to the sales venues shaped to fit consumer society.[7] But above all, in these revisited spaces, the museum becomes the space of the theatre, the spectacle for a media-dominated society.

The cave essentially expresses the idea of a magical place, in which messages and images are engaged in indirect relations. The transformed places thus come back to speak to us of this mystery, between the contemporary image that is increasingly destabilizing and the back wall, which becomes the screen for new tales.

With installations, art leaves the conventional museum to enter the conflictual space of life. But in the corroded and corrupt places, whether industrial or having served other functions, the art of our time finds the perfect setting for dialogue, absorbing the aura of unease emanating from these places.

After having passed through the myth of the transparency of the modern world, the ideals of a democratic interchange between inside and outside, today the museum encounters the theme of opacity, of a rupture of the one-to-one relation between interior and exterior, between building and city, between space and exhibition, between individual and society. If, for the architects of the Modern Movement, material had to be reduced to a minimum of information to the point of becoming transparent, today in the post-industrial society, in which the messages of art invite us to reflect on the crisis of our times, the wall is no longer the frame or the window through which we can observe the outside world, but rather the place in which the multiplicity of information of our time stands out, in an intermixture of codes. Material in these time-worn bodies, in which the museum is established, becomes the projecting surface of Plato's cave, where the new images of the contemporary age encounter the reflexive light of the past.

[1] Regarding the theme of the museum as an urban system: Pippo Ciorra, 'Dalla "città-museo" al "museo-città",' in Pippo Ciorra, *Botta, Eisenman, Gregotti, Hollein: musei*, Electa, Milan 1991.

[2] Regarding the work in the 1980s and 1990s by international architectural culture, see Antonino Saggio, *Peter Eisenman. Trivellazioni nel futuro*, Testo&Immagine, Turin 2005. As Saggio points out, the transformation in Eisenman's concept of frame in the Wexner Center for the Visual Arts relates to the rereading of the works of Giuseppe Terragni, who had exalted in his works the spatial principle generated by a dynamic elaboration of structure. In the book, the author clarifies a change of direction regarding both methodology and composition in the construction of the space of the museum.

[3] On the relation between architecture and the media: Robert Venturi, *Complexity and Contradiction in Architecture*, The Museum of Modern Art Press, New York 1966. With respect to the historical and critical position in Italy—that same year Aldo Rossi published *L'architettura della città* and Vittorio Gregotti *Il territorio dell'architettura*—Venturi's writings challenged the orthodox thinking of modern architecture, including the interference of the media. On the contrary, in Italy the historical idea of the city and a new alliance between territory and geography was still the focus of attention.

[4] For further reading on the transformation in art between the 1940s and 1960s introduced by Informal Painting and Abstract Expressionism, see Yve-Alain Bois, Rosalind Krauss, *L'informe: mode d'emploi*, Centre Georges Pompidou, Paris 1996; and Rosalind Krauss, *Reinventare il medium. Cinque saggi sull'arte di oggi*, Bruno Mondadori, Milan 2004.

[5] Regarding the new conception of the body, free of social conventions, read Gilles Deleuze, Felix Guattari, *Anti-Œdipus. Capitalism and Schizophrenia* [1972], vol. I, Athlone Press, London 1984. The text challenges psychoanalytic theory, analyzing the body as a rewritable surface. The philosophers shift attention to desire and away from the need which had marked Freud's theories. The body translates into a *desiring machine*.

[6] For an understading of the relation between myth and the contemporary era: José Saramago, *A caverna: romance*, Caminho, Lisbon 2000. Regarding the theme of the shadow, I mention two essays explicitly analyzing the question in art: Ernst H. Gombrich, *Shadows. The depiction of cast shadows in Western art*, National Gallery Publications, London 1995; Victor I. Stoichita, *A short history of the shadow*, Reaktion Books, London 1997.

[7] Regarding the deconstruction of the museum as an institution, see Federico Ferrari, *Lo spazio critico*, Luca Sossella Editore, Rome 2004.

Interweave

UN Studio
New Mercedes Benz Museum

Frank O. Gehry & Associates
Guggenheim Museum

Coop Himmelb(l)au
Akron Art Museum

Steven Holl Architects
Kiasma – Museum of Contemporary Art

Michael Maltzan Architecture
Fresno Metropolitan Museum

Daniel Libeskind
Denver Art Museum

Daniel Libeskind
Royal Ontario Museum

Zaha Hadid Architects
The Lois and Richard Rosenthal Center for Contemporary Art

Delugan Meissl Associated Architects
Porsche Museum

Diller Scofidio + Renfro
Eyebeam Museum of Art and Technology

Zaha Hadid Architects
Maxxi National Centre of Contemporary Arts

UN Studio
Extension Te Papa Museum

Nieto Sobejano Arquitectos
Contemporary Art Centre Córdoba

Steven Holl Architects
Herning Center of the Arts

Mansilla + Tuñón Arquitectos
Musac – Contemporary Art Museum of Castilla y León

Twentieth century art history opens with the passage from Impressionism, which defined its spaces with the help of new scientific discoveries in the field of optics and where everything was transmuted into perceptions of light, to Expressionism, which anticipated the traumas of the First World War and shifted the artist's viewpoint from the outside world to the inner world of the individual. The birth of this current, which introduced the overwrought dimension of decomposition, ushered in a new conception of space and matter. The memory, which gets its sustenance from interweaves in an involuntary and synesthetic dimension, has modified the interpretation of traditional museum spaces. Helixes, weaves, Möbius strips, and upward spirals are the spatial principles introduced into these new complex organisms. In this view, the museum is no longer a neutral space that preserves, but rather a site where purposes and contradictions come together and interrelate. The spatial dimension prevails over its material counterpart, connections over simplicity, the container over the content. The museum itself, like a magmatic substance, is transformed into a work of art, shaped by the expert hands of a master glassworker. Here we enter the field of a Foucaultian heterotopia, i.e., into spaces endowed with multiple meanings. The interweave that such museums evoke encounters multiple and varied identities and gains sense within a space that gets its nurture from new relations. The indistinct and the homogeneous, principles upheld by Modernity, give way to the dissimilar and the multiple. Space wins over the work, the interweave over linearity. The void becomes the raw material of the museum-interweave, the substance that makes it possible to incorporate diversity into the admixture, since all conclusive or categorical dimensions are excluded. The expressive museum transforms into a journey in which it is the continuous changes of route that give meaning to a contemporary memory that exists in dialectical contrasts, in open and continuous settings. The observer becomes a time traveller, ready to be astounded by the spatial traps that the accomplished hunter has laid.

2006
Stuttgart, Germany

A new museum for Mercedes Benz has been built along the B14 highway. It represents a new philosophy of museographic space based on the Möbius strip: a ribbon which, folding onto itself, continuously generates an alternation of one- and two-storey spaces. The museum accommodates a store, a restaurant, offices and a lofty lobby opening upward all the way to the top floor. The site is landscaped with an artificial hill, making the entrance visible to travellers on the B14. The pathway through the museum starts at the top level and then descends along ramps that intertwine in a way that is reminiscent of a strand of DNA. This freedom of movement makes it possible for visitors to choose their own personal programme and constantly shift their vantage point. The large internal opening adds to the scenographic qualities of the experience and ensures the fortunes of this extraordinary visual machine.

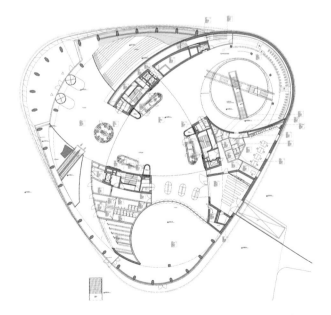

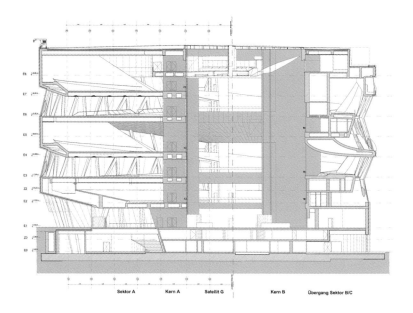

Sektor A   Kern A   Satellit G   Kern B   Übergang Sektor B/C

Frank O. Gehry
& Associates

Guggenheim Museum

1997
Bilbao, Spain

Built in a former industrial area where the city meets the river, the museum
appears to be driven along the urban trajectories by a dynamic inner force.
A bridge over the Nervión links the Guggenheim to the Bilbao suburbs on the
north side of the river. The architecture is generated by a dilation of the masses,
like a futurist work. The power of the new organism is immediately felt inside the
entrance atrium. There is a spectacular sense of space with a vertical cut rising
some fifty metres. The atrium leads to the various functions, which include a
small auditorium, restaurants and shops. The museum eludes any definition or
interpretive limitation. It is a work of art itself, on a par with its contents, and in
many ways it vies with them. It is precisely in this turning of the tables that
Gehry's work poses new questions as to the nature of this time-honoured
institution.

Akron Art Museum

2007
Akron, Ohio, USA

The museum was built in Akron, Ohio in response to the need to expand the exhibition spaces of the pre-existing institution. It is a glass and steel machine that re-evokes futuristic, aerospace landscapes and science fiction movies. Inside the space is dynamic, interwoven and technological. The futuristic component combines with a mental and surreal counterpart. The building is composed of three parts; the Crystal, a multipurpose space for artistic or other events; the Gallery Box, an exhibition space shaded from natural light; and the Roof Cloud, which tempers the natural light and creates shaded outdoor areas. This spacious wing evokes images of flight and embraces and protects the pre-existing brick building. The design reminds us of the metaphorical and symbolic function of the new contemporary arts institution: that of creating a bridge among historical periods.

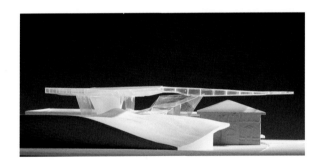

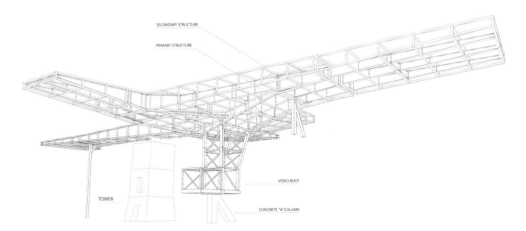

Kiasma – Museum of Contemporary Art

1998
Helsinki, Finland

Situated north of Helsinki in an area characterized by a fragmented morphology, a nodal point between the old city and the early 20th-century suburbs, the museum seeks to reunite these diversified expressions of the city's urban and social history. What is produced is one of the buildings that has best succeeded in fusing space within the aesthetic conception of an interweave. Years after having visited Le Courbusier's La Tourette, Holl succeeded in giving material form to the idea of the excavation in this urban organism that emerges from the Finnish city. Kiasma is formed by the fusion of two bodies and two ideas. A sinuous form faced in zinc panels is grafted onto a rectilinear block made of glass and aluminium. This project has exemplified the infinite potentials of contemporary architecture. Here Le Corbusier's promenade becomes a material that strongly shapes the interior space and especially the exterior of the building. Well integrated into the city's history, the museum gives a strong character to the urban space.

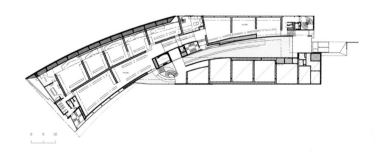

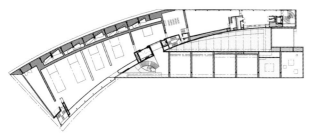

Michael Maltzan
Architecture

Fresno Metropolitan Museum

2002
Fresno, California, USA

The permeable and evanescent form of the new museum seeks to create new public spaces in its interconnections with the pre-existing structure. At the plaza level, these niches are carved out by erosion of the architecture that shapes itself around a void space. The exhibition areas are characterized by flexibility and continuity of their open spaces. Below them, pools of water have been designed to cool the summer heat and create a pleasant microclimate for the public. The roof, adapted to the presence of photovoltaic panels, supplies the building with energy in the winter. The museum transforms into a climatic project implemented on the basis of the idea of interweaving functions which underpins the project philosophy. The form is folded over like a continuous ribbon, a mass shaped to fit the surface of the city.

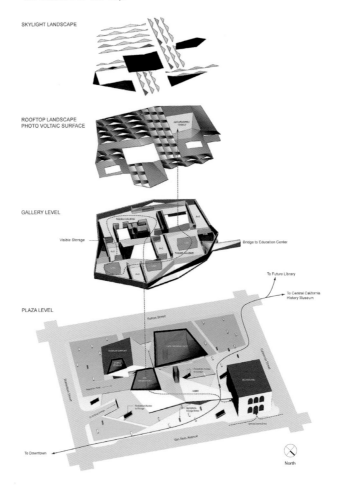

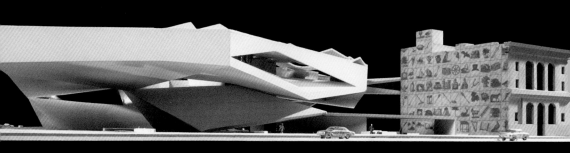

Daniel Libeskind   **Denver Art Museum**

2006
Denver, Colorado, USA

The museum, developed as an extension of the one designed in 1972 by Gio Ponti, accommodates the functions of the main hall, a bookshop, a cafeteria, exhibition spaces and a theatre. The entrance atrium provides access to the various functions. The paths fold back on themselves in this scenographic and fluid space that constitutes a visual representation of the concept of continuity. The colossal steel frame is faced in Colorado granite and titanium. The form is bold, spectacular, dynamic, incisive. Thanks to technology, the space lives in a world where gravity is practically absent. It is architecture's response to Surrealism. The Denver Art Museum exerts an attractive force on the observer and conveys a sense of mutated form, which changes with vantage point. It is a memory machine that inhabits an upside-down reality.

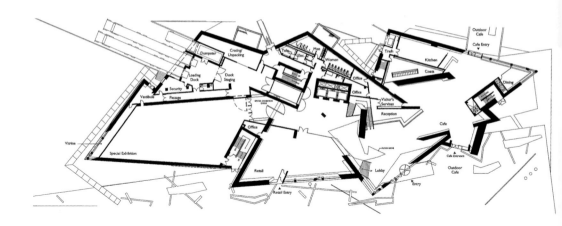

Daniel Libeskind   **Royal Ontario Museum**

2007
Toronto, Canada

The building is generated out of a geometry of buddings. Two metaphors meet in the Canadian city: the crystal and the desert. In anchoring itself to the pre-existing structure, the museum enters into conflict and tension, rising like a massive prism out of a desert. The large windows in the façade provide glimpses of the inner workings of this baroque machine. Diagonal walkways cut across the space at different levels in the hall. The Royal Ontario Museum is conceived as a contemporary *Wunderkammer*, the German cabinets of curiosities that once contained a multitude of objects in their rooms, including the earliest machines, instilling an extraordinary sense of wonder in visitors at the time. The ROM provides a new interpretation of the theme of suggestion and magic.

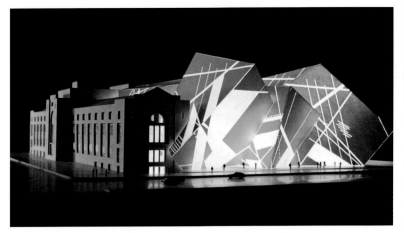

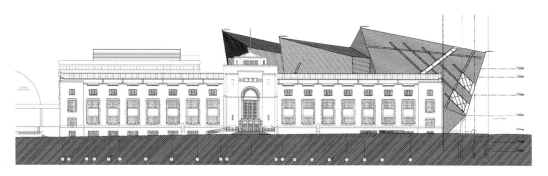

Zaha Hadid Architects

The Lois and Richard Rosenthal Center for Contemporary Art

2003
Cincinnati, Ohio, USA

The museum was ideated as a place of interchange in keeping with the current views on spaces for contemporary art. The project originates in agreement with the principles of the historical avant-garde, futurist and Russian suprematist movements. The work presents an animated façade that appears ready to detach or to evolve, conceptually, into a new figure. Incorporated into the heart of the city, it becomes the pivot point in a network of relations between institutions and art lovers. Inside, the back wall is shaped like a curved sheet accommodating a scenographic ramp. In virtue of these variegations, the museographic space is conceived so as to generate unexpected and dizzying perspectives. Art is extended from the two-dimensional work to a set of environmental relations. The rooms vary in form and size in order to offer the visitor a diversity of experiences. The interior spatial continuity extends outside onto the façade as a sort of cubist architecture.

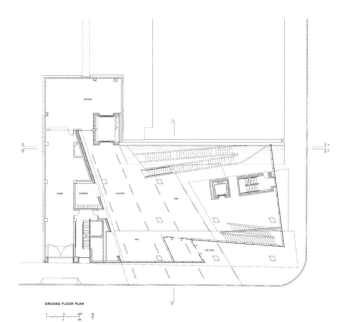

GROUND FLOOR PLAN

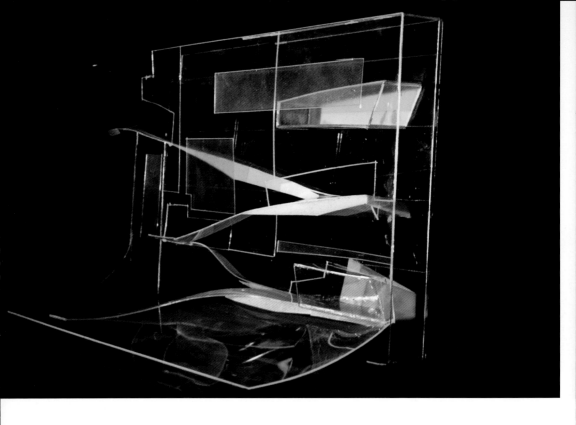

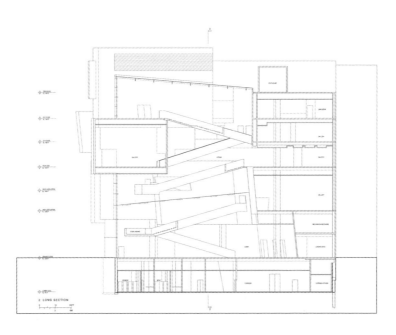

2 LONG SECTION

3 CROSS SECTION

Delugan Meissl
Associated Architects

Porsche Museum

2008
Stuttgart, Germany

A monolithic structure will become the new museum for Porsche motor company in Stuttgart. Conceived in keeping with the modern vision of museographic and entertainment facilities, the museum will have restaurants and shopping areas. The interior appears to be shaped by the action of pressure and generates a sense of movement along a series of ramp-platforms. Detached from the ground, the museum is a three-dimensional structural machine whose aerodynamic form evokes the aesthetics of speed. The building shapes itself to fit the city and its urban design, but refuses to interact with the ground. The plaza is created with inclined planes that give a scenographic quality to the public space. The monolithic and closed image transmitted by the exterior gives way to the changing slopes of the platform-exhibition spaces inside and transmutes into a feeling of open space that invites interrelation.

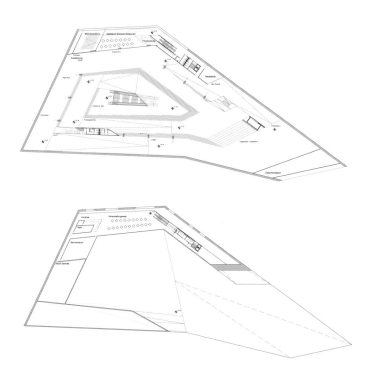

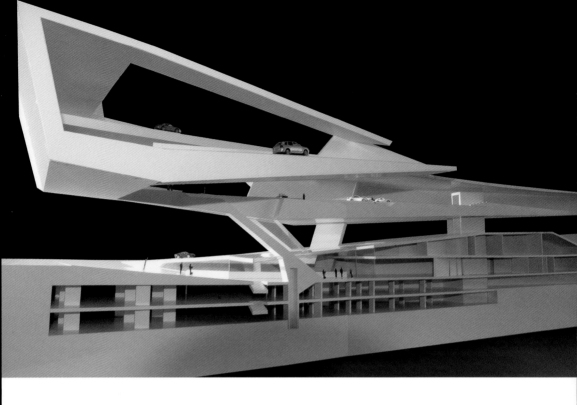

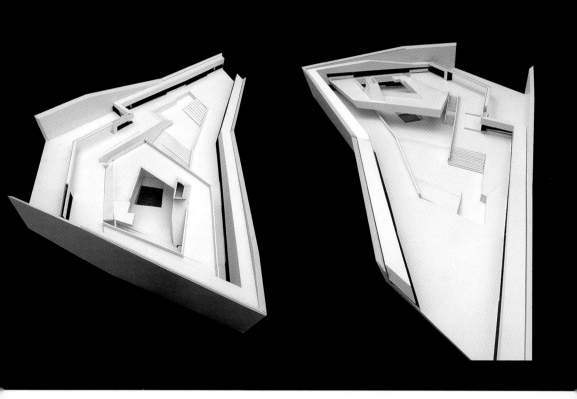

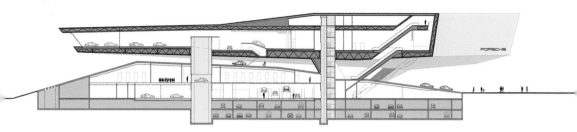

Diller Scofidio + Renfro   **Eyebeam Museum of Art and Technology**

2004
New York, New York,
USA

The Chelsea neighbourhood of Manhattan, home to many major art galleries, will be the site for the Eyebeam Museum of Art and Technology. It is a curved ribbon, like a Möbius strip, and in the philosophy of these years it exemplifies an interwoven place of interchange. In the mind of the architects, the intervention seeks to create a continuous space that folds back on itself to create 12 floors. The aim is to bring together in dialogue the production spaces (atelier) with the presentation spaces (museum, theatre) so that there will be cross-contamination among the experiences of different operators and the public. The museum of new multimedia technologies clarifies its technical potentials within its own skin. Indeed, the outer membrane will contain all the technical and electronic plants for the building, which will transmute into an architecture of information.

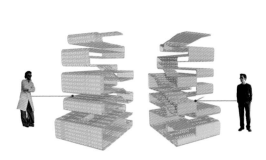

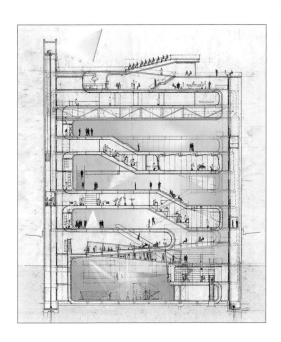

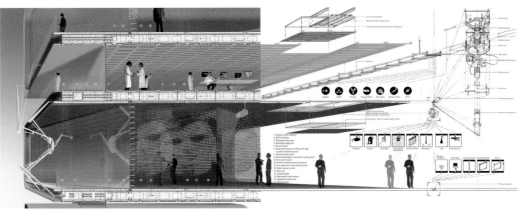

Maxxi National Centre of Contemporary Arts

2010
Rome, Italy

Conceived as a second skin for the site, the project excludes the idea of being grafted onto the pre-existing structure and instead stands as a new spatial process for its context. It gives visual form to the spatial and functional ramification in a way that is reminiscent of the method for twisting rope. It appears as if the urban infrastructures had been raised, generating a recessed identity for the site. In this quest for fluidity, the Centre for Contemporary Arts is self effacing as an objective presence and instead seeks a relationship with its surroundings based on circulation vectors and forces. The pathway through the museum thus seeks to fragment the modernist vision of a neutral cube and generate in the observer an inclination to relate the space to the work in keeping with the new paradigms of contemporary art. Here, we encounter an altered idea of space and time with respect to that embodied in the 19th-century museums.

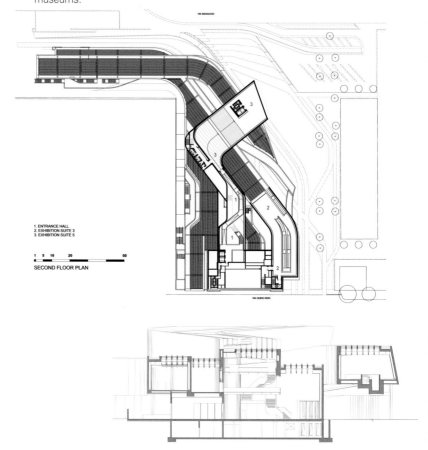

1. ENTRANCE HALL
2. EXHIBITION SUITE 3
3. EXHIBITION SUITE 5

1 5 10   20   50

SECOND FLOOR PLAN

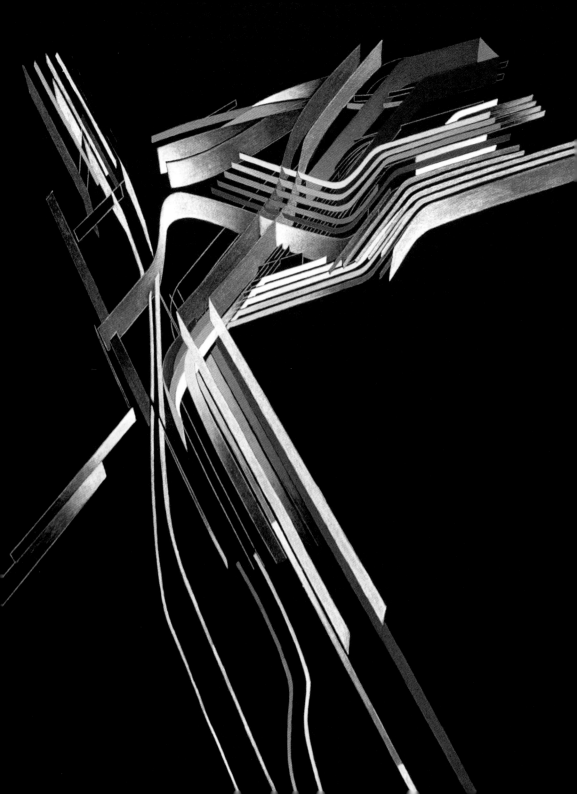

Extension Te Papa Museum

2005
Wellington,
New Zeland

The intervention joins a plan to transform the city of Wellington spearheaded by the project to redevelop the waterfront. The proposed building rises from the ground and structures itself as two paths that intersect to inform the museum's interior and exterior. It is a shaped surface that re-evokes the process of design, introducing architecture into a close kinship with a pursuit of plasticity. Inside the museum, the path denies a frontal view in favour of ambient and relational perception, so that large works can be assimilated from a distance, as can the sculptures placed at different heights and in different positions. In addition to containing art, the museum itself is a producer of aesthetic processes. The external space, shaped like a folio, accommodates small open-air concerts and presentations.

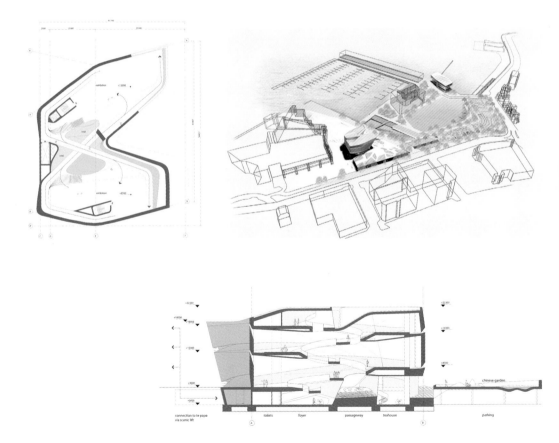

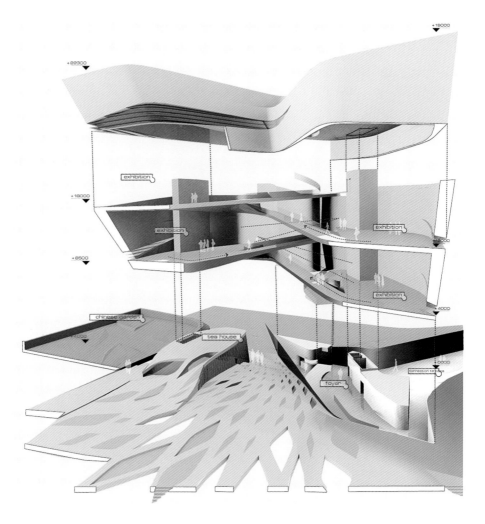

+22300

+18000

exhibition

+18000

exhibition

exhibition

+8500

exhibition

+13000

chinese garden

+4000

tea house

foyer

connection terrace

±0000

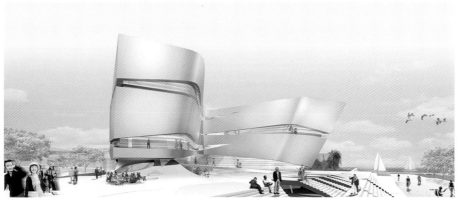

Contemporary Art Centre Córdoba

2005
Córdoba, Spain

The project recovers the echoes of Hispano-Islamic memories from the weave of Cordoban culture. The Contemporary Art Centre, adhering to the creative and artisanal aspects of architecture, has been conceived in diametric opposition to a rigid, closed geometry, to a neutral and global container. Instead, the sumptuous richness of the space of mosques has inspired the development of a complex spatial system whose geometry is based on hexagons of different sizes connected together into a weave informing both the programmes and the internal relations. The workshops border on the exhibition areas, producing an idea of the museum as a meeting place for different actors. The side looking over the Guadalquivir River transforms into a screen perforated by luminous LEDs. The museum aspires to being a centre of creativity and a workshop for expressivity.

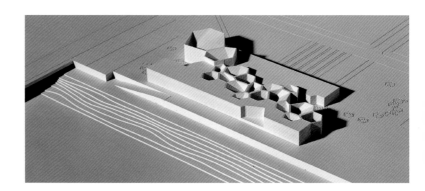

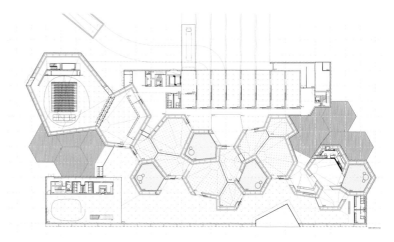

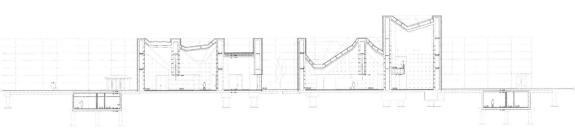

Herning Center of the Arts

2005
Herning, Denmark

This museum seeks to generate a landscape, transforming the site into pools of water, and to shape its masses as if by the hand of an artisan. The curved roof creates contoured sections for the entrance and for the diffusion of light. The galleries are delimited by orthogonal bearing walls that create an essential space for exhibitions, while the internal partitions can be moved to allow flexible arrangements. The museum is oriented around the geometrical spaces of the galleries and extends in a series of tentacles that generate trajectories across the landscape. These elements may translate into passages, into strokes across the land, or into access points to the museum. A double dimension of both rule and expression prevails in this work. A design for geothermal climate control marks this as an environmentally sensitive project.

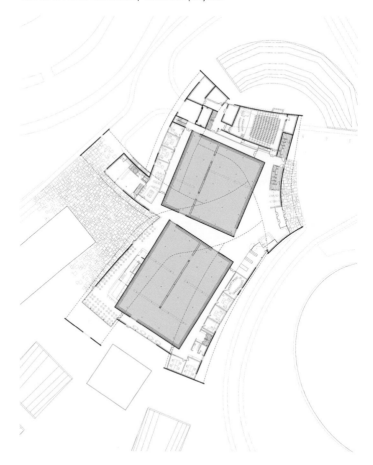

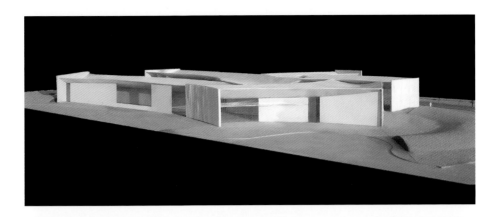

Musac – Contemporary Art Museum of Castilla y León

2004
León, Spain

This project represents a museum and workshop rolled into one, a facility for exhibitions and also installations, theatre performances and concerts. The plan evokes the idea of a spatial interweave with a geometry of clustered diamonds reminiscent of medieval patterns. Here continuity is the matrix that generates the interior space in a weave that invites one to seek diagonal internal pathways. With its intense colours inspired by the stained glass windows of the cathedral, the exterior conveys an image of the museum as a place for meetings and interrelations. Inside the space becomes rather bare: stone and concrete are the main materials. The beams exalt the constructional qualities. Large skylights of varying dimensions allow light to enter the internal nodes. They also provide a way to vary the spaces by changing the light capture system. The expressivity of the colour in the plaza is juxtaposed with the silent and intimate qualities of the interior.

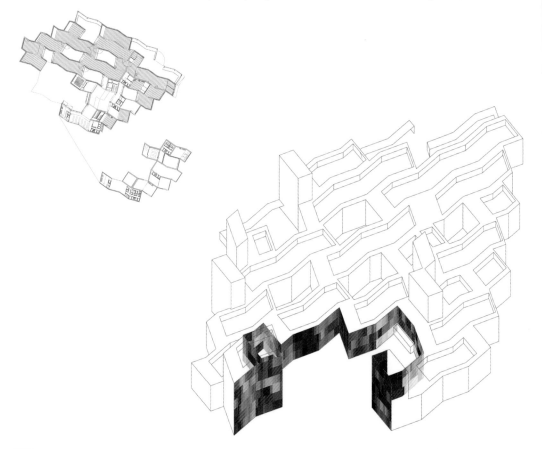

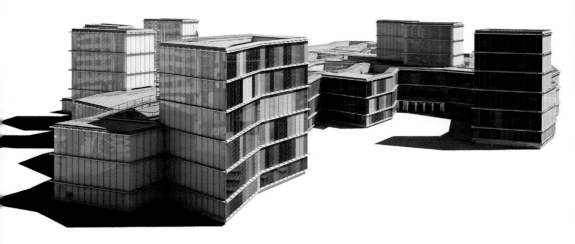

Theatre

What is a scenic machine? Why does the contemporary age come into contact with the theatre, the space in which the relation between man, the social context and the divine order has historically been perpetuated? It is, first and foremost, a place that creates a buffer zone between reality and representation that is still capable of inspiring us to reflect upon the relationship between the self and eternity. It is a fertile, stimulating venue that lives in virtue of the ephemeral time of the Universal Expositions, or an ambiguous space such as that which measures itself against the changeable substance of water. These museums are the dwelling place of the temporality of vision. Memory is no longer a realm that is perpetuated potentially ad infinitum. On the contrary, it inhabits a relative timeframe. In this dimension the eye is activated, it is stimulated by the occurrence of the event. Space is no longer something represented within but rather the mirror of an external realm. The site and the context experience a new interaction created by the museographic installation. Within this temporal dimension, the external space is transformed, it changes substance. A ritual is created that shifts the mind of the observer into a new consciousness which then produces a new critical vision. If the museums that are established on the waterfronts of industrial cities carry within their very substance the colourless presence of water and its evanescent and fluctuating qualities, for the pavilions erected in the expos, the space immediately becomes scenographic: the venue accommodates the new presence for the relative duration of its life. And yet, paradoxically, these museums of temporalized vision aspire to eternity. The time that they evoke is without confines, in many ways abstract, and calls forth principles that cannot be located in time or in space. While its material constitution is destined to expire when the moment of its representation has run out, the awareness that the time allotted to the museum is destined to be brief makes these new venues of the contemporary age particularly attractive: it is a memory that is consummated in an intense and fleeting recollection.

Diller + Scofidio   **Blur Building**

2002
Yverdon-les-Bains,
Switzerland

One of the most interesting ventures in recent years was built over Lake Neuchâtel in Switzerland: a pavilion evoking the tensile structures of Buckminster Fuller that suddenly vanishes into a cloud. Thanks to a computerized system of 31,500 mist nozzles, the pavilion draws water from the lake and atomizes it to create a dense, concealing shroud of mist. The effect varies constantly with the wind changes and the external atmospheric conditions. The theme of blurring, both disciplinary and visual, opens the field to a new idea of memory and context involving material, information and landscape. The cloud hides everything even from the surveillance of telecameras. With this project, which calls back into play our other senses and ability to orient ourselves in a visually indistinct environment, memory is transformed from a visual experience into a synesthetic one.

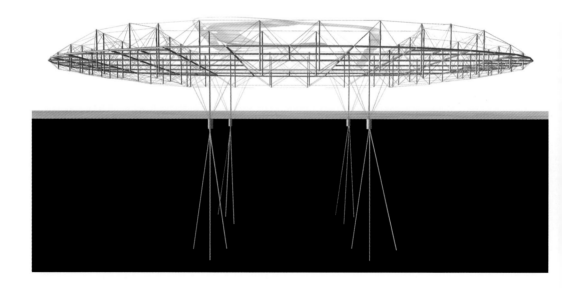

Coop Himmelb(l)au   **Expo 02 Forum Arteplage Biel**

2002
Biel, Switzerland

Created for Expo 2002 at Arteplage Biel, the three towers orient and mark the terminus of a walk along the lakeside quay. They are three totemic machines. Transparent, they bend and deform to generate an intermixture between the image of solid geometry and that of dynamic plastic forms. The three elements, varying in height from 35 to 43 metres, create a palpable tension while standing as symbols of something both informatic and archaic. At night the three towers transmute into landmarks, luminous beacons whose steel frames faced in microperforated panels are transformed into an evanescent architecture engaged in dialogue with the water. The pavilion converts the landscape into an open-air museum and imbues the view with relativity, in which time is determined by the duration of the event.

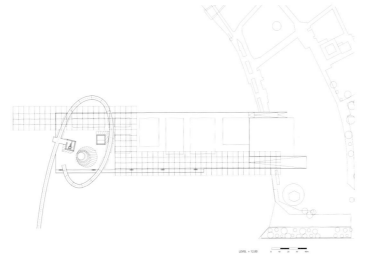

LEVEL + 12.00

Hydrapier Pavilion

2002
Haarlemmermeer,
Netherlands

The Hydrapier Pavilion falls into the scenic machine category of museum. It is a structure waiting to be able to move along the artificial lake near the Dutch town of Haarlemmermeer. Conceived as a sort of boat, the project exalts the perception of the landscape, where the image of the museum as an enclosed and protected showcase is replaced with one that is projected outwards. With its steel frame, it becomes a metaphor for movement. The town was founded in an area that was below sea level until the 19th century, on a site that was drained some 150 years ago. In the scenic space both the roof and the glass walls are touched by flowing water and evoke the memory of this place and machines such as pumps, dikes, which gave the town the land upon which it stands. Museum-land-memory fuse naturally in this small project.

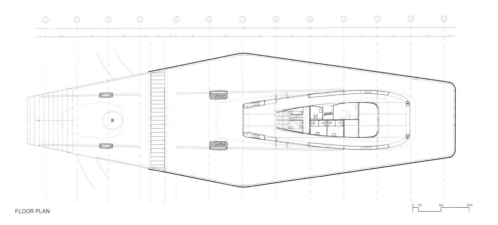

FLOOR PLAN

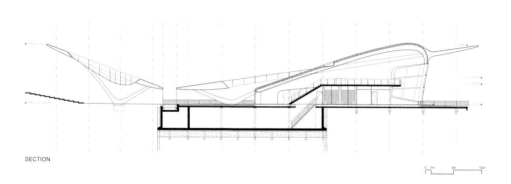

SECTION

Coop Himmelb(l)au

Groninger Museum – The East Pavilion

1994
Groningen, Netherlands

The Groninger Museum originated as part of a programme to renovate the museographic institution in the heart of the Dutch city of Groningen. The goal was to send out a new message whereby the building demonstrates its fealty to the arts, itself being transmuted into both an object and a generator of communication. Adhering to the formal principles of deconstruction, the pavilion decomposes and deforms in an architectural process of splitting in direct dialogue with the water. The interior museum, penetrated by aerial walkways, declares its allegiance to the designs of Piranesi in a dynamic spatial flourish. Water becomes the factor of attraction and the museum dialogues in refined contact with the ebb and flow of the sea. In the form and syntax of its volume, the pavilion evidences its interdisciplinary nature, in keeping with the eclecticism of the collection of works on display.

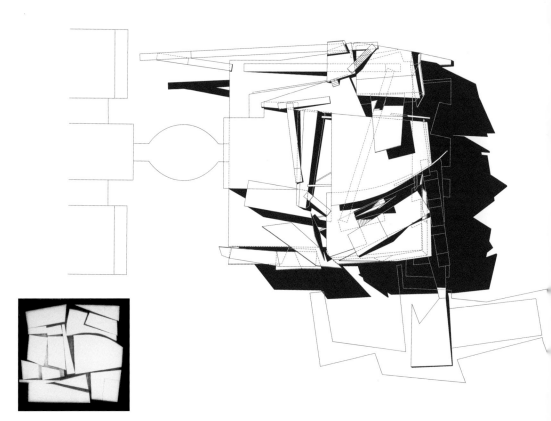

Bianimale Nomadic Museum

2005
New York, New York,
USA

A nomadic, itinerant museum, ephemeral in its construction technique, was built in the New York harbour in 2005. It is a project that enquires into the permanent-evanescent dichotomy. Constructed on Pier 54, famous as the planned destination for the Titanic's ill-fated maiden voyage, it is composed of a stacked array of 148 shipping containers. It is 205 metres long and 4 files of containers high, circumscribing an area of some 4000 square metres. Inside, a colonnade was built using 64 tubes of pressed paper 75 centimetres in diameter spaced at intervals of 6 metres. They support a truss made of the same material with a diameter of 30 centimetres. While the materials are innovative, the space they create is reminiscent of a classical temple. Externally, the containers are positioned in a staggered manner to create a dynamic view from the side. Diagonally mounted curtains create interesting shadow lines. The structure can be easily disassembled and is ready to take form anew in its next port of call.

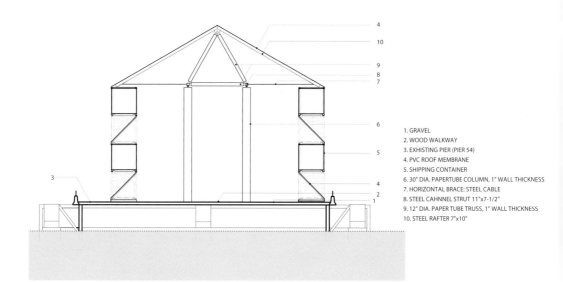

1. GRAVEL
2. WOOD WALKWAY
3. EXHISTING PIER (PIER 54)
4. PVC ROOF MEMBRANE
5. SHIPPING CONTAINER
6. 30" DIA. PAPERTUBE COLUMN, 1" WALL THICKNESS
7. HORIZONTAL BRACE: STEEL CABLE
8. STEEL CAHNNEL STRUT 11"x7-1/2"
9. 12" DIA. PAPER TUBE TRUSS, 1" WALL THICKNESS
10. STEEL RAFTER 7"x10"

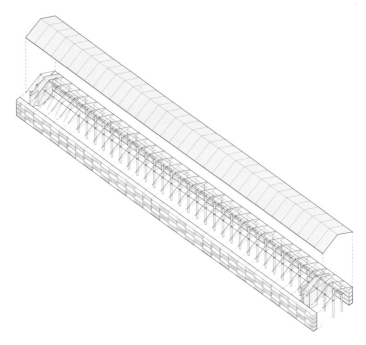

Coop Himmelb(l)au   **Musée des Confluences**

2001
Lyon, France

The Musée des Confluences will be built at the confluence of two rivers, the Rhone and the Saone, at the edge of an industrial area, which is slated for radical transformation. The location has conditioned the nature of the project, which seeks to generate a sort of contemporary public space, one that is compact like a boat and fluid like the rivers with which it is engaged. It is a machine that shapes itself by mutations of form and telluric movements to create an internal landscape. The result is highly scenographic spaces for which the broad plate glass windows at the entrance, opening toward the city, create a strong point of attraction. The lobby is conceived as a sort of public square that generates a variety of different perspectives. The exhibition halls embody a preference for complexity and spatial interweaves within this contemporary machine. It is a museum from the age of information, simultaneity and interactivity for a society in constant movement.

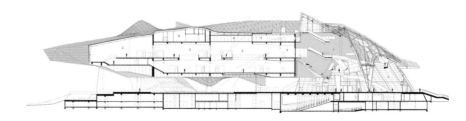

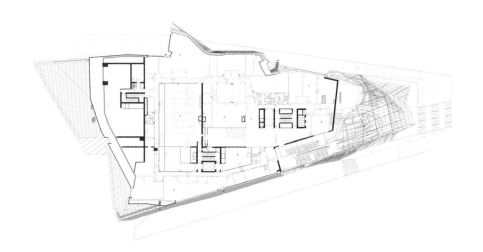

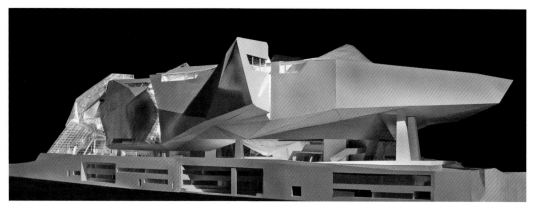

Rudy Ricciotti

Musée National des Civilisations de l'Europe et de la Méditerranée

2004
Marseilles, France

The museum is a perfect square, standing in front of the Fort Saint Jean in Marseilles in one of the most intensely historical and cultural areas. The façade is richly textured materially, in opposition to the clichéd choice of transparent surfaces. The project communicates the idea of erosion and dematerialization. The square form measuring 72 metres on a side contains within it another measuring 52 metres, the heart of the museum. The building is engaged in a close relationship with its site, avoiding any dialectic with the historical city. In the harsh and enduring landscape marked by the local limestone and the presence of the fort, the new project offers an evanescent image, like a reticulated membrane that exhibits its flying structures. Ramps lead the observer to views of the sea landscape. A terrace, open to the public, turns the museum outwards, towards the time-honoured realms of the city's history.

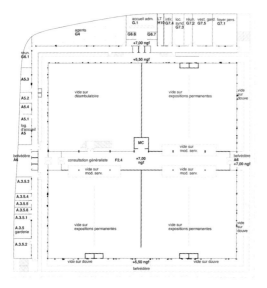
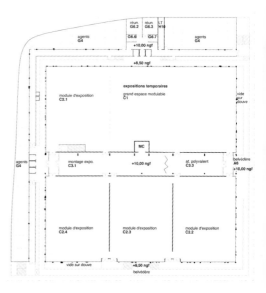

277

Jean Nouvel   **Classical Museum**

2007
Abu Dhabi,
United Arab Emirates

This project seeks to re-establish contact with the culture of its context. It is a fascinating work for its essentiality and oneiric references, and for its interwoven structure and transposition of light, which filters through the material of the building. A sense of fluidity dominates. The buildings are arranged around broad platforms of water, while the translucent shell-like roof evokes the ramifications of trees. It is a suggestive design which works with natural elements in an agreement between formal simplicity and exaltation of climatic factors, dictated by the interdependency between the intense heat of the location and cooling effect generated, with the help of the wind, by the broad internal pools.
A Mediterranean landscape is invoked in the museum spaces. The works of art will fulfil the task of bringing colour into this extreme space.

Daniel Libeskind

Imperial War Museum North

2002
Manchester, UK

The Imperial War Museum North was built in the harbour of the city of Manchester. It recounts the horrors of war and seeks to lay out a visual planetary geography: the crust of the earth that deforms, creases and fractures under the action of internal and external forces provoked by human violence. It is a project in which symbolic, metaphorical and spatial values join and fuse. The entrance is notable for its soaring, striated structure through which one enters the museum with its two exhibition halls, shops and cafés. The spiral circulation layout allows visitors to move according to personal design or whim. The museum includes multimedia installations and vintage films that guide the observer into a tormented realm. The presence of military planes, tanks and original documents from soldiers offer a vivid image of the horrors of war, in keeping with the intentions of the architect.

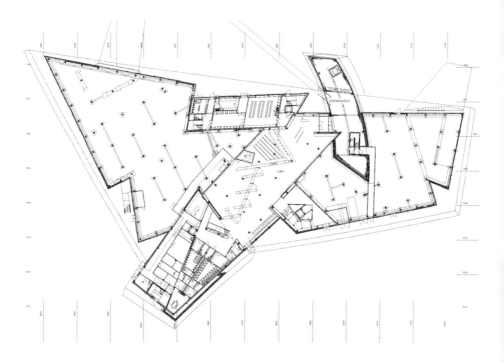

Institute of Contemporary Art

2006
Boston, Massachusetts,
USA

On Fan Pier, south of Boston, the Institute of Contemporary Art measures itself against the dynamic nature of the water and the waterfront. The overhanging structure interweaves exhibition spaces, a theatre, a mediatheque, bookstore, shops and a restaurant in an integrated plan. Conceptually, the museum represents a folded piece of paper, a structural slab that generates the theatre and the exhibition hall. The recessed ground floor provides access via a wide ramp to the interior of the museum. The mediatheque is projected toward the water, almost seeming to risk falling in. The physical and visual top of the building is the exhibition hall. It is surrounded by a system of lenticular windows that allow you to see out only at right angles, while the view is blurred from other vantage points. In this dimension, artworks, environment and landscape create new dialectical relations.

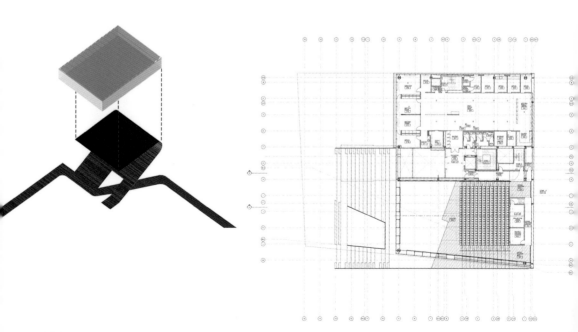

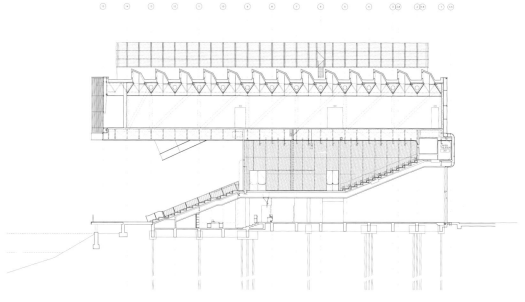

The New Museum Contexts

The policy of museums has found a new relationship between memory and setting in recent years, a relationship growing out of the far-reaching revolution sparked by philosophy and especially by art. In order to comprehend this new dimension it is necessary to get an overview of the transformations in the interpretation of the landscape, whence descends the way of conceiving museum space, which transmutes into an outwardly oriented optical machine.

If we consider the museum to be an expression of a broader way of feeling, if we think of it as the venue for events, we can agree that Hadrian's Villa in Tivoli, built in the 2nd century CE, is one of history's first museum-like expositions. Today it presents itself as a mysterious place, a place of ruins, with parts solidly anchored to the ground, resisting the passage of the centuries. The walls record ancient construction techniques but also and especially the visionary genius of Hadrian, who had his curiosities and travels carved into the now ancient stones. Hadrian wanted his villa to incorporate everything he had experienced on his ventures. And so we see a return of Greece of the Acropolis, with copies of the statues of the caryatids of the Erechtheum in memory of the structural function of the body, and Egypt of Alexandria, with the Canopus evoking the space of the Nile delta. Like a contemporary listing on an ancient matrix, these are places whence re-emerge the theatres of the past. The villa has also represented a place of encounter for all time travellers. Ever since the era of the Grand Tour, it has represented a destination for pilgrimages for its wealth of history and culture, for its constant and eternal quality of being both interior and exterior.

In 1776, Giambattista Piranesi would make a painstaking survey of the state of the ruins, with the plants that had taken root among the fallen stones and crumbled vaults. Using the constructive rules of past times, the etcher gave us a vision of the parts that had collapsed over time, where the ruins continue to speak to us of memory, a contemporary memory. Hadrian's Villa is a landscape in which Hellenist and Roman culture intermix. It is a space that has been shaped, but never flattened into a *tabula rasa*, that brings together east and west into one. The museum site *par excellence*, it is still today a theatre where the past and the present coexist and are able to offer new strategies for the future. Here architecture and landscape form an indissoluble whole.[1] Nature has been shaped by the masterful ways of engineering. Today, this museum of memory, which has suffered the attention of time, returns to nature, it is slowly being consumed to remind us that the landscape is also an intermixture of historical, anthropological, cultural and social time and certainly also witness to the passage of time as etched by the atmospheric elements.

The landscape changes over time. It changes because societies, engineering techniques and especially worldviews evolve. If the ploughshare is the instrument that has historically marked the land and created a territory of furrows, lines and interweaves, with the combinatory rationale of the crops characteristic of the Middle Ages, the soil too is crafted as a collage. The Renaissance, in a reinterpretation of the Roman *hortus conclusus*, designed the gardens of villas with a strong symmetry and regularity. Nature, in the reassertion of reason and the central importance of the individual, was bent to human will and shaped according to a superior principle and order. The 17th century inserted the idea of movement into the landscape, of acceleration via the formal and centrifugal dynamism of space. In the 18th century, in keeping with the nascent aesthetics of the sublime, nature, landscape and memory were interpreted within a broader acceptation: they are the manifestations of forces that act inexorably on humankind, beyond any possibility of interaction. The sublime introduces aspects of the terrifying, gigantism, of a non-reconciliatory power. Veduta artists portrayed scenes of earthquakes or lava flows from an active volcano that overpowered humans' vain certainty of control.

The relationship between museum and territory witnessed a new interpretation toward the end of the 19th century with the birth of open-air museums, which had the purpose of evidencing the cultural and anthropological history of the location. The Skansen Museum, created in 1891 on Djurgarden Island near Stockholm, ushered in the idea of preserving the local farming culture that was disappearing under the onslaught of the transformations wrought by the industrial revolution. Among the goals of its founder, Arthur Himmanuel Hazelius, was that of recovering similar settings that he considered authentic in various parts of the Swedish territory. It was the first open-air museum, the prototype of a model that would be successfully developed in northern Europe and North America. Material culture became a new focus of attention. Some villages and farmhouses were moved and rebuilt. These museum-villages or living museums met with extraordinary success in America, generating over time a policy for the preservation of local and territorial culture, in which history and legend are brought back to life in virtue of their appeal to a new sort of tourism. It was a trend that sought to unite the provision of leisure-time activities with an educational component, a concept captured in the neologism 'edutainment.'

The 20th century brought a phase distinguished by strong acceleration in industrial development that witnessed a makeover of the city's exterior. The countryside and undeveloped areas became zones of conquest, transformation, consumed by the new demands of modernity. The landscape lost its autonomy and transmuted into industrial settings where new organisms—factories, mines, warehouses, infrastructure, rail bridges—modified and marked the land. Hence, over time the need grew to reinterpret these factories, some having roots reaching back into the first wave of industrialization in the 18th century, a wave that had swelled to a veritable tsunami in the twentieth. This transformation generated the need to seek out new places of memory, isolated places, in which nature reigns supreme.

The great art patrons sought out suitable contexts for setting up museums as outposts, tesserae in a utopian mosaic.

It was the industrialists Anton Kröller and Helene Kröller-Müller, husband and wife, that would create a new model for a museum in relation to the landscape. They wanted to build a gallery for their large collection of art in a park or on a country estate. In the first phases of the project in the years 1911–14, architects of the calibre of Peter Behrens, Ludwig Mies van der Rohe and Hendrik Petrus Berlage were invited to submit plans. The final choice of locating the Kröller-Müller Museum in Otterlo, Holland in the De Hoge Veluwe natural park was the work of the architect Henry van de Velde. It was a context that would create a shadow line across which modern art could dialogue.

The museum, completed in 1938 by Van De Velde, is a structure composed of enclosures of differing height in a stable and austere composition of volumes enclosed in the wooded garden, which would become an open-air exhibition area for different artists ranging from Dubuffet to Fontana, and from Rodin to Moore.

In parallel, while museum architecture generated spaces that were still well defined, the great transformation in the view of the landscape was brought about in the first decades of the 20th century by artists who began to interpret the external world in a two-dimensional, mental, translated way. It is enough to turn one's gaze to all of abstract painting, from Kandinskij to Klee, from Mondrian to Albers, and from El Lissitzkij to Malevich. The season of the historical avant-garde movements opened the way to a new way of conceiving the inextricable relationship between inside and out, between nature and artifice, between museum and landscape.

Kandinskij had hypothesized a theory of composition based on the triad of point, line and plane, three conceptual, physical, territorial and vectorial structures of forces that spark action. But it was Klee who ideated a way of thinking about the territory as a project of real and imaginary lines, fabrics and weaves. We now see the relationship between the museum and its context translated into formal and figural principles thanks to the literature of artistic abstraction, which has played a fundamental role in advancing a new interpretation of the landscape that requires a project of recognition and unveiling.

Today the territories are less marked. They exist in a condition that increasingly tends to be less delimited, and the border as well becomes less strongly pronounced. Ian McHarg expressed a keen intuition in referring to the landscape as an unstitched canvas.[2] It was an idea of cohesion and continuity in which the gridwork, the corrugated material, the valleys are all combined into a continuum. We enter an interpretation that took form in the second half of the 20th century as a result of social, cultural and political changes against the background of a renewed interest in the environment.

New trends emerged in the 1960s and 1970s in the United States, which was modifying the global order, prodded by the media against the background of a revolution that embraced a new view of the body as a tool of investigation in Body Art and Fluxus, but especially in the Land Art of Richard Long, Robert Smithson, Walter De Maria, or Michael Heizer, who considered land and the landscape to be an interweave of relations, on which one could write, transcribe, leave marks or construct new rites. We are in a phase of human history when the themes of saving the environment, introduced earlier by Richard Buckminster Fuller and Frederick Kiesler in the *Manifesto of Correalism*, published in 1949 and promoting the idea of integration between art and nature, were becoming increasingly pressing and a matter of public concern. Over time, the public became increasingly aware of this view of the landscape, following all the episodes of wanton exploitation of the land and its resources, technology-related accidents, oil spills, the destruction of the Amazon rain forest, etc.

The Land Art movement had brought interest back to an idea of a place in which the human presence interacted in that context with accidental, minimal signs. Thus all the errant literature returned, the archaic dimension of nomadism, walking as a cognitive process. This is the dimension of the *flâneur*, who found his loftiest literature in the 20th century, from the Hebraic writings of Walter Benjamin and Paul Celan to those of the Briton Bruce Chatwin, who impersonated the figure of the intellectual-nomad. His writings allow us to reinterpret the territory as a travel experience, a route, a path. His work became the fulcrum of a new way of recounting and assimilating contexts, but above all, the writer was able to descend into the caverns of myth to show us the origin of things.

Chatwin tells us in *The Songlines*, published in 1987 that 'The names of the brothers are a matched pair of opposites. Abel comes from the Hebrew "*hebel*," meaning "breath" or "vapour": anything that lives and moves and is transient, including his own life. The root of "Cain" appears to be the verb "*kanah*": to "acquire," "get," "own property," and so "rule" or "subjugate." "Cain" also means "metal-smith." And since, in several languages—even Chinese—the words for 'violence' and 'subjugation' are linked to the discovery of metal, it is perhaps the destiny of Cain and his descendants to practise the black arts of technology.'[3]

The writer helps us understand the distinction between sedentary culture, which has shaped and bent nature to its will, and nomadic culture, the culture of flows, which found a synergetic relation with its territory. Chatwin leads us to a new vision of the world as a flow of experiences and knowledge. The walkabout allows us to perceive other dimensions, encountering and combining different cultures and information.[4]

Today, thanks to a renewed sensitivity to ecological issues, museum and context design passes back over the traces of archaic civilizations in which mud and rocky concretions have generated a new aesthetic in the imageries of the artist and writer-traveller. Moreover, Body Art and Land Art defined a relation between body and space that from this point on would be inextricable. The landscape exists in virtue of the subject that, by moving through it, maps it, marks it, personifies it.[5]

If we investigate the process-oriented nature of the work of land artists, we may understand many lines of pursuit that have now flowed into contemporary museum architecture.

The works of Richard Long, such as *A Line Made by Walking* (1967), Michael Heizer, including *Displaced, Replaced Mass* (1969), or Robert Smithson, such as *Broken Circle/Spiral Hill* (1971) make it possible to re-establish an extraordinary contact with the primordial signs of archaic civilizations. Additionally, this current has created a true antecedent in that it is an art form that is, in the final analysis, transmissible only via the instrument of photography, thus signifying a parting of ways in our time between memory, the duration of the event and the *temporality of vision*. In 1969 the movement was made public via a television special 'Land Art' directed by Gerry Schum. The works of these artists, ephemeral in terms of material resistance, could be frozen, captured only in the instant of the filming; the work disappeared with the end of the shooting.

In 1970–72, Richard Serra built his work *Shift* in King City, Ontario. In a meadow, the American artist designed some broken walls based on the idea of the transformation of the land. The work has the dual function of transcribing onto the land the movement of two people who orient themselves and lose sight of each other because of small variations in the land contours. Serra thus introduces a dual theme associated both with movement and with the perception and idea of the body, a body that reads, maps and modifies the territory by means of its action.[6]

These expressions give us the seed of a way of intervening in the memory of places via pressure, routes, directrices, accidental signs in a material that is both a process and substantially linked to the infinite time of nature. In spite of the fact that many Land Art practitioners hailed from minimal art, the movement runs distinctly counter to the metropolitan images of serial, geometrical monoliths that constituted the cages and primary structures of Minimal Art. On the contrary, the land artists recovered both the materials and the processes by which they interpreted the artistic action from the land.

We owe to this season, which had found in the American landscape a new synergy with nature, a renewed interest in the concept of time, which is not the time that passes day-by-day but rather that which passes with the millennia, which modifies the context via a slow, inexorable action. Paradoxically, this ephemeral art found itself framed in the desert territories, suspended and without gravity.

This new attention to the environment, growing out of the climate of political renewal in the 1960s and 1970s, led to the birth of the Ecomuseum, an expression coined in 1971 by the museologist Hugues de Varine. It was a phase of historical revision that emerged and developed in 1982 with the *Nouvelle Muséologie*, which moved the bond of memory from the interior walls of a museum to the land and to the community that nurtured both. Tradition, environment, and transformation are the principles to preserve and protect.

While the open-air museums considered the site to be a social experience and a cultural asset to be defended, the Ecomuseum shifted the principle of protection of relics to that of the defence of assets, in the broadest acceptation of the concept of land. This embraces both nature as an unquestioned asset and the anthropogenic environments, the settings modified by humans. The idea of the Ecomuseum takes memory back to the community where it was born, into the spaces of a new sociality.

Like the artist who eliminates the nature of the easel and the studio to create art in the natural context, so the museum abandons the walls of the galleries to translate itself into a new concept of environment. In parallel, conceptual art and post-structuralist philosophy broke up a number of principles associated with a past image of memory and power. A new sociology arose in different fields, in literature as in art.

Certainly the *actions* of Joseph Beuys took us into a new mode that interpreted memory as a social action in space, within an idea of process. In Naples in 1981, following the earthquake that caused deep damage in the city, he created his installation *Terremoto in Palazzo*. Within the scenic space, he used everyday objects recovered from the culture of the place, from the open-air garbage dumps. The performance highlighted the land of Campania, subjected over long centuries to the alterations and transformation caused by earthquakes and the activity of volcanic areas. Hence the tables, the household objects of a timeless life, rested on glasses, and in the corners they supported, in an unstable equilibrium, vases or other objects. It was a way to sustain a labile identity: a territory subject to a fatalism caused by a magmatic vision lacking in stability. And so the museum became the interpretation of existences, dreams, a metaphor for unease.[7]

In Kassel in 1982, he ideated a living installation (*7000 Oaks*) as part of the famous *documenta 7* exhibition, in which he designed within the city, which transformed into a museum over an indeterminate span of time, the replacement of 7000 basalt stones with oak trees. The project grew out of the desire to experiment with the theme of ecology. The artist pushed the inhabitants to undertake a conscious action, in *adopting* an inanimate material such as basalt in favour of a tree, sign of life. It was his desire to transform the heart of the historical city into a living and animated landscape. It was only with the aid of people that he could create his work of art. Beuys invited the city dwellers to reflect on themes that today are vital. He transgressed the temporal limits of the artistic action in a collective rite that could last for centuries. Furthermore, Beuys affirmed the idea of a society of artists, evoking ancestral rites in his role as shaman, scapegoat or martyr.[8]

Art and literature invite us into a complex territory of accumulations and superimpositions, and combinatory actions. This is the space into which Georges Perec leads us. In a period of some ten years he penetrated into consumer society and etched out a window through which to go beyond the confines. In 1965 he published *Les choses. Une histoire des années soixante* [*Things. A Story of the Sixties*] in which he tells the story of a couple who are literally absorbed and swallowed up by everyday objects, the expression of a transformation of the world into goods. Perec describes places with an obsessive capacity for detail, cataloguing and enumerating. The places transform into contexts that assume an existence that is almost independent of the subject who lives in them, but at the same time make them human, like a transmission of sentiments from the subject to the object, like a projected shadow. When he published *Espèces d'espaces* [*Species of Spaces*] in 1974, the narrator analyzed all possible spaces: the bed, the neighbourhood, the city, the countryside and the nation. The space and the place lose their characteristics of stability and sedentariness and become potentials, settings in which reality is often uninhabitable, in which the interweave prevails, in a narrative intended as combinatory art. Space loses its autonomy and must constantly be interpreted, analyzed, and invented. In the first few pages of the book, Perec writes, 'In short, spaces have multiplied, been broken up and have diversified. There are spaces today of every kind and every size, for every use and every function. To live is to pass from one space to another, while doing your best not to bump yourself.'[9]

In his writing no direct relation is achieved between space and subject, as if they were two beings that in the final analysis are alien, that live through exchanging their respective existences. This underground world became the manifesto of the book published in 1978, *La Vie, mode d'emploi* [*Life: A User's Manual*], which describes events associated with a building in Paris, analyzed in section as if vivisected. The spaces and rooms hide a drama, a mysterious tale in which reality is ramified. The one hundred rooms, like the stories recounted, are actually excavated burrows in which, as if in a combinatory process or a puzzle, the tesserae compose themselves with others in an uninterrupted flow, sundering the linear relation between space and time. The places are no longer seen as unique, but take on the colours of the infinite combinations to which the story subjects them.

This dimension was preannounced and investigated by the philosopher Michel Foucault, who identified the birth of these heterogeneous spaces in the moment in which history and power are not considered unique and self-referential forms. When we can define a plurality of stories and powers then we enter the world of differences, where in a single place we can juxtapose 'sites which are irreducible to one another and absolutely not superimposable on one another.'[10] The French philosopher identifies the theme of the crisis, 'the heterotopia begins to function at full capacity when men arrive at a sort of absolute break with their traditional time.'[11] Hence the heterotopia is not understood to be a temporal figure, but a stage in which the present experiences a crisis of conscience.

As Foucault sees it, 'The museum and the library are heterotopias that are proper to Western culture of the 19th century'[12], in which we find the accumulations of all possible times at a single time in a single space. The dimension of plurality against the homogeneous and indistinct (themes associated with the utopia of the modern era) opens up questions of the relationship between physical space and the individual's inner space. We enter a sphere in which our inner being is also interpreted as a landscape.

Thus stated Michel Foucault in Tunisia at the *Des espaces autres* [*Of Other Spaces*] conference in 1967: 'The space in which we live, which draws us out of ourselves, in which the erosion of our lives, our time, and our history occurs, the space that claws and gnaws at us, is also, in itself, a heterogeneous space.'[13]

From different standpoints, with Beuys, Perec and Foucault, a conventional view is negated of place, which dramatically penetrates into the subject as a multitude of differences, coming to stand for the complexity of life. The idea disappears of a place with roots, that which the museums, from those of material culture to ecomuseums, had tried in different ways to keep alive. The crisis point in consumer society, initiating at the close of the Sixties, is the end of the idea of the original, as Walter Benjamin had much earlier stated in his essay *The Work of Art in the Age of Mechanical Reproduction*. This time has denied the principle of authenticity.

But excavation, like erosion, are processes that from time immemorial have shaped the land.

Foucault's theses have now found their way into all possible literatures, thanks partially to the work of Gilles Deleuze, whose 1988 text, *Le pli - Leibniz et le Baroque* [*The Fold: Leibniz and the Baroque*], opened the way to new possible interpretations starting from the dynamic, concave and convex world of the Baroque. Space, both existential and physical, is interpreted as a fold, which, capable of unfolding and folding again *ad infinitum*, generates the idea of a constantly rewritable surface, in keeping with the thesis of the psychologist Lacan regarding the weave of the mind.

The philosopher identifies the fold with the theme of reversibility, like a space that can constantly be reshaped, whereas the furrow, which is inscriptive in nature, is permanent. The land is considered to comprise a thousand superimposed layers, stratified, various. The metaphors regard the themes of mountains and rocks, sedimented, in which different heterogeneous substances have accumulated and compose a new coherence among the parts. We have thus passed from an idea of the landscape as a collage of homogeneous material components to the idea of a *post-collage*, something that is inclusive, that upholds superimposition as models for a new alliance between nature and artifice, in which the limits and the layers merge together.

In the 1980s, the prevailing trend was a reading of the site and its *genius loci*, as a memory-informing identity, in which the deity of the place imprinted upon it a distinctive character, along the lines of the theories developed by Christian Norberg-Schulz. In the next decade, the landscape was understood as a palimpsest, as a place of archaeological stratification.

It is no coincidence that the relationship between the context and the museum now involves a new interpretation of the land: think of Burri's *Cretto* in Gibellina, which indeed reshaped the mountain, or Peter Eisenman's works for Santiago de Compostela, which started from the diagrams of the lines of the historical city and interprets the project as an act of algebraic modelling of the site.

Today the museographic operations on the landscape are nurtured by this literature, which is philosophical above all, and which is implemented via new instruments and new interpretations. The museum in an outdoor context must necessarily reflect this new interpretation of place, permeated as it is with an idea of the spatial, mental and geographical movement of a new nomadic subject.

In 1990 it was Rem Koolhaas who offered us, with his unbuilt project for a Convention Centre in Agadir, a clear interpretation of the theme of the excavation. The year marked, as we have said, a line of demarcation between an interpretation of the museum and the city associated with a structural and urban memory, and one that elaborates the project, in its external areas, as a process of excavation in a landscape that is at once archaic and contemporary. The Agadir project would influence all subsequent literature, opening the field to the idea of an eroded platform conforming to the contours of the land and in tension with the setting, the site of differences. This material is considered as elastic, flexible and conformable as the ground itself. As a consequence, in the 1990s a new way of interpreting the museum and the landscape as non-separable places was theorized.[14] The theme of the land is that which we read again today in the new projects by Brückner & Brückner, Steven Holl, Productora, Tezuka Architects, Alvaro Siza, and Mansilla + Túñon.

The museum enquires into places that normally would have been considered marginal or excluded areas, such as the abandoned quarries where Brückner & Brückner realized one of their most interesting works. Granitmuseum Bayerischer Wald in Hauzenberg is an integral part of the stepped excavation, of the hewn lithology. The project re-establishes a connection with the very substance from which it draws nourishment. Artifice and nature settle together, nurtured by one and the same gesture.

Within this material excavated by humans, these slabs crafted by the rational use of the extraction machinery and the rationale of transformation of the quarry, the museum generates a sense of continuity. It uses the same material, as in the processes of Land Art, the same rationale of function as a part of a whole, the consequence of an identity. Site and context thus become a single body, a sole substance.

In this view, nature is no longer seen as benign, an object of contemplation, but rather as the dynamic space in which transformations and modifications occurring over time have altered the equilibria. This is Gilles Clement's interpretation in his *Manifesto on the Third Landscape*, which introduced a new way of seeing the land in which the sites abandoned by humans have generated marginal places that are much richer than they might otherwise have been in an environmental and biological sense. The landscape itself is translated into a process.[15]

The museum grows out of its context or creates its context, as in what ranks as one of Alvaro Siza's boldest and most interesting projects, where he modelled an eroded, shaped, hollow mass. In the Iberê Camargo Museum in Porto Alegre, the Portuguese architect interpreted the nearby mountain and drew from it an image of shaping that he infused into the sinuous form of the new museum. Siza interpreted the context, the mass of the mountain behind it, the light that finds its way into its hollow body, where the connections detach themselves from the interior and assert their formal autonomy in the forthright material of unfaced cement. But above all, the museum evokes the visionary and tormented world of the artist Iberê Camargo in a rereading of his existence and place.

Mansilla + Túñon, winners of the design competition for the Cantabria Museum, are the authors of one of the most fascinating works of the current generation. It is not a work on the ground nor an annulment inside the maternal womb, but a rereading of a natural landscape.

In 1975 the artist Richard Long travelled to Nepal and captured a series of images that testify to an enduring territory, one that is mythological in certain ways. The eroded, dynamic, corrugated, faceted form of the rocks shaped by a slow, millenary process, was, in the artist's mind, already an expressive work. These rocky mountains reconnect us to the cycle of life, to an ever renewing energy, to circularity as the place of dreams and origin of life. The Argentine writer Jorge Luis Borges, in his short story *Las ruinas circulares* [*The Circular Ruins*] relates the magic circle to the creation of life. It is the story of a man who seeks to create another human being from his own dreams, discovering in the end that he himself is the offspring of a dream. The author reminds us of the birth of the myth and the imagination.

The new generation of architects approach the composition of the landscape through new instruments, which derive not only from a direct analysis of the site but also through the mediation of photography, such as that used by land artists. Specifically, the images produced by Richard Long have defined a mental landscape, a mindscape, that has been translated into the space of the museum. The megalithic stones of the Minoan culture or Easter Island, the *nuraghe* of Sardinia, or the extraordinarily evocative stones of Bernard Rudofsky's book, *Architecture without Architects*, are all part of a new aesthetic that establishes a relation between the natural and the artificial, memory and land. In his book, Rudofsky shows us the archaic and legendary locations of Egypt or the excavated architectures in Göreme, Turkey and the Libyan fortresses in the Cabao Formation. Mansilla + Túñon's Cantabria Museum brings back the stone architectures of the past, the contemporary sense of the excavation, erosion, adaptation to the land, shaping, and the construction of dwellings inside rocky masses.

So the idea of the museum hinges on a dual paradigm: a transcription and translation of the signs of land art, and a reinterpretation of rocky lands, testimony to a looming, granitic, lithic nature that opposes the duration of time with its ability to resist and endure.

The museum includes the land as a founding actor, as a space of observation.

But if we move out of the external territories, with which the museum seeks to interact and establish an identity, and enter the theatrical spaces of the Universal Expositions or museum-exhibits, we find ourselves in a special sphere and a new idea of landscape. Here the limited time of the event determines a new type of memory. This time has been, in the final analysis, institutionally associated with duration, resistance. The massive architecture of the past testified to the need to preserve that time. With the *temporality of vision*, the observer becomes the main actor in a new museographic phenomenon. Memory is no longer interpreted as an absolute, as a grey-matter constant. On the contrary, this new dimension introduces us into a time in which the relationship between the exterior-landscape and the interior-memory comes up against a fragmented vision, one that grows out of the interferences between the real world and the mediated one. In this acceptation, there is no longer a sharp distinction between exterior and interior. No, this process that shifts museum architecture from act to event, from *factory* to *machine*, necessarily gives rise to a new time factor, in which not only is the event temporalized, but the very structure of the museum-pavilions exists only for the minimal duration of the exhibition.

What happens in this new interpretation and what tools do we have to comprehend it?

We must introduce two settings that are useful for understanding what is happening: the *Panorama* and the *Panopticon*. These are *machines for seeing* that originated in late 18th-century English culture, specifically, both were invented in 1787. The Panorama, literally 'total vision,' was a painting on a cylindrical surface patented in 1787 by the English painter of Irish ancestry Robert Barker, who built a two-storey rotunda in Leicester Square, London in 1793. The observer entered this optical machine through a dark covered passage and stood on a platform to observe the 360° scene surrounding him or her on all sides. It was a machine that anticipated the cinema and proposed via its panoramic view, the illusion of a three-dimensional image. The scene was changed from time to time, from urban scenes to scenes of natural settings, with the illusion of being out in the open surrounded by spectacular nature.

In parallel, Jeremy Bentham described and structured the idea of the Panopticon, etymologically 'the eye that sees all,' in 1786–87. The Panopticon was a multi-level prison radially arranged around a central point. From a cylindrical tower in the centre, the guard had a 360° view and could exercise total surveillance over the prisoners. The English jurist and philosopher was convinced that this monitoring would improve the disciplinary nature of the inmates. While the Panorama introduced an illusionistic perspective, the Panopticon, analyzed by Michel Foucault in his book *Surveiller et punir: Naissance de la prison* (1975) [*Discipline and Punish: The Birth of the Prison*], brings us into the society of control. Both dimensions characterize this time period in which the rituals of entertainment and surveillance dictate our social dimension. While the Panorama is the subject that exercises power over the landscape, in the Panopticon, it is power that acts on the subject.

This dimension of contemporary memory, of the museum as a mindscape, was analyzed by the American architecture studio Diller Scofidio + Renfro, the creators of the Blur Building on Lake Neuchâtel in Yverdon-les-Bains: a pavilion that disappears into a cloud of mist. The architects designed an elliptical platform of notable dimensions: 100 × 60 × 10 metres at a height of 15 metres above the lake and evoking a Buckminster Fuller geodesic dome. The large structure is governed by a computer that controls 31,500 high pressure mist nozzles fed by water from the lake. There are different interpretive routes, all oriented toward the psychological and sensory perception of the visitor. The museum becomes an interactive work of art that makes the stable substance of the lake into something pulsating through a indefinite blurring that obscures the limits of the real.

The experience is translated from visual to sensory when the visitor enters into the fluctuating platform. The vaporized cloud makes the visual experience indistinct and blurred. For the architects, the atmospheric conditions translate into a global, universally comprehensible theme. They introduce an unqualifiable dimension, something that cannot be measured, leaving to the weather and the winds the possibility of varying the mass, consistency and nature of their invention.

The modern space of the body, represented by the metaphor of the machine, is transformed into the electronic body. Blur immerses us in a dimension of indistinguishability. Concepts such as near-far, inside-outside lose their meaning. Once in the building, visitors feel disoriented due to an alteration of their normal way of perceiving: there is nothing to see except their dependence on seeing. In his 1999 book, *Mémoires d'aveugle* [*Memoirs of the Blind*], Jacques Derrida explores the theme of blindness in the history of painting. In his conception, the image is not the point of arrival but a threshold beyond which to see and which at the same time shows us our blind spot. Derrida makes it clear that vision can no longer be satisfied with sight alone, but requires a transfer toward the other senses: hearing goes farther than the hand, which goes farther than the eye.[16]

In Yverdon, Diller and Scofidio interpret the landscape as a folio and use the water to cause a crisis of sight to produce, as the architects themselves state, an anti-heroic architecture, a low-resolution technology, as indefinite as a cloud, by using the most advanced systems technology can offer to amplify the atmosphere of uncertainty caused by the mist. Here technology is used against itself. Memory, space and information enter the virtual dimension. The formal has dissolved into the sentient. It is the landscape, liquefying itself, that acquires an autonomous and disquieting, palpitating and pulsating life.

In Yverdon-les-Bains, the context is also transformed into an event, a performance event that modifies both space and existence in the instantaneousness and temporality of sensation. Museum and context merge into an interactive relationship, in which sight loses its vocation for memory. The Blur Building annuls panoramic vision, since the obfuscation denies control of the view outside, and panoptic vision, since the telecameras cannot capture or recognize images in this blurry dimension. No power and no monitor can impose a condition of surveillance in this machine of the senses. At this last frontier, museum and memory are no longer iconographic milieux but invoke the mental time of emotions, in which the external landscape disappears and one enters an indistinct space where it is one's senses that act as a guide through one's inner landscape.[17]

[1] For in-depth reading on the landscape and the construction of the imperial residence at Tivoli, see William L. MacDonald, John A. Pinto, *Hadrian's Villa and its Legacy*, Yale University Press, New Haven 1995.

[2] A reconstruction of various ways of interpreting a site is discussed in Franco Zagari (ed.), *Questo è paesaggio – 48 definizioni*, Gruppo Mancosu Editore, Rome 2006.

[3] Francesco Careri, *Walkscapes. Camminare come pratica estetica*, Einaudi, Turin 2006, p. 13. The text analyzes the concept of the landscape as a journey and crossing-through. And I also mention Bruce Chatwin, *The Songlines*, Penguin Books, New York 1987.

[4] For an understanding of the idea of landscape as a nomadic action, see Bruce Chatwin, *In Patagonia*, Penguin Books, New York 1977.

[5] On these themes I recommend the chapter 'Land Art, Process Art, Arte Povera,' in Francesco Poli, *Minimalismo, Arte Povera, Arte Concettuale*, Editori Laterza, Rome-Bari 2009, pp. 121-156.

[6] On the relation between art and land, see Michael Lailach, *Land Art*, Taschen, Cologne 2007.

[7] For further reading on the intense relationship between art and society, see the catalogue *Terrae motus*, Electa Napoli, Naples 1984. In the introduction, Giulio Carlo Argan captured the dramatic nature of Naples: 'Its Mediterranean space is flooded with light, but from one moment to the next, the earth may tremble and Vesuvius spew forth torrents of fiery lava' (p. 17). But it was Joseph Beuys to place a dramatic focus on the relation between the tragedy of the earthquake and the need for social redemption. He wrote: 'The tremors are still shaking the buildings. The physical jolts in the many towns and cities of southern Italy and in Naples itself—with the many dead, of whom we must think if we want to bring about radical transformations—are nevertheless to be put in relation with the continuous, indescribable collapses of the buildings of western private capitalism and eastern state capitalism' (p. 24).

[8] Regarding the role of the artist in political action: Joseph Beuys, Michael Ende, *Kunst und Politik: ein Gesprach*, Freie Volkshochschule Argental, Wangen 1989.

[9] Georges Perec, *Species of Spaces and other pieces*, translated and edited by John Sturrock, Penguin Classics, London 1998, p. 6.

[10] Translation from the Italian: 'diversi luoghi che sono tra loro incompatibili,' Michel Foucault, *Eterotopia. Luoghi e non-luoghi metropolitani*, Mimesis Edizioni, Milan 1994, p. 16.

[11] Translation from the Italian: 'l'eterotopia si mette a funzionare a pieno quando gli uomini si trovano in una sorta di rottura assoluta con il loro tempo tradizionale,' *ibid.*, p. 18.

[12] Translation from the Italian: 'Il museo e la biblioteca sono eterotopie tipiche della cultura occidentale del XIX secolo,' *ibid.*, p. 18.

[13] Translation from the Italian: 'Lo spazio nel quale viviamo, dal quale siamo chiamati fuori da noi stessi, nel quale si svolge concretamente l'erosione della nostra vita, del nostro tempo e della nostra storia, questo spazio che ci rode e ci corrode, è anch'esso uno spazio eterogeneo,' *ibid.*, p. 13.

[14] For an overview of the evolution of the museum, see these two texts: Michele Costanzo, *Museo fuori dal museo. Nuovi luoghi e nuovi spazi per l'arte contemporanea*, Franco Angeli, Milan 2007; and Stefania Zuliani (ed.), *Il museo all'opera. Trasformazione e prospettive del museo d'arte contemporanea*, Bruno Mondadori, Milan 2006.

[15] Regarding the interpretation of marginal areas and their potentials today, see Gilles Clément, *Manifesto del Terzo Paesaggio*, Quodlibet, Macerata 2005.

[16] Jacques Derrida, *Memoires d'aveugle: l'autoportrait et autres ruines*, Reunion des musees nationaux, Paris 1990. I also recommend two essays on the same theme: Paul Virilio, *Esthétique de la disparition*, Balland, Paris 1980; Paul Virilio, *L'art à perte de vue*, Galilée, Paris 2005. A final dialogue may be useful for understanding the new aesthetic dynamics, found in: Enrico Baj, Paul Virilio, *Discorso sull'orrore dell'arte*, Elèuthera, Milan 2002.

[17] For an understanding of the relation between landscape and memory within the information revolution, see Antonello Marotta, *Diller + Scofidio. Il teatro della dissolvenza*, Edilstampa, Rome 2005. I also mention a number of books that have highlighted a new way to think of the relationship between form and dissolution in art and literature: Honoré de Balzac, *Le chef-d'oeuvre inconnu* [1831]; Giovanni Papini, *GOG* [1931], Stabilimenti Grafici Valsecchi, Florence 1945, pp. 131-134. Issues relating to control have been examined in philosophy and sociology. I propose two key texts, which, years later, show the changes associated with the system of information control: Michel Foucault, *Surveiller et punir: naissance de la prison*, Gallimard, Paris 1975; David Lyon, *The electronic eye: the rise of surveillance society*, Polity Press, Cambridge 1994.

Context

The museum has transformed recently in the acquisition of context. It has transformed from a place endowed with multiple vantage points and interpretations into a new dimension that lives and breathes in relation to the site that has generated it. It is no longer the city with its urban measures and generative axes that determines the boundaries of the project or its social image. The museum-context arises in marginal areas, abandoned quarries or in places where nature reigns supreme, deriving its measure and its logic from the new context. From ecomuseums to their open-air counterparts, these works emerge as projections from the landscape. Nature and the environment are no longer interpreted as disjoined processes. On the contrary, the natural and the anthropogenic contexts constitute a single organism that the museum institution seeks to protect and clarify. In this acceptation, the new museums are stimulating general interest, bringing back to life many projects that had found a new alliance with nature in art, such as the geometrical abstractions of Klee and Kandinsky and later the Land Art of the 1960s. Today this attention to the pattern and weave of the landscape, and respect for the environment, finally finds expression in the very fibres of the museum. These designs do not turn for inspiration to the abstract, serial grids of Minimal Art, but recover the more innovative sense of Land Art. As a consequence, the museum finds its life in the natural lines of the site, it responds to the contours, settles into and adapts to the context in which it takes form and with which it seeks to coexist in a synergetic relationship. It is not a question of container and contents: the memory aspires to a transmutation into nature, abstraction seeks to become process, seeing the site and surrounding environment as rightfully parts of the legacy to be preserved. In this sense, the works to protect are the lands with their particularities and specificities. The museum becomes a watchtower and beacon light that defends their borders.

Brückner & Brückner   **Granitmuseum Bayerischer Wald**

2005
Hauzenberg, Germany

The museum is located in the extensive Bayerischer Wald near Hauzenberg, Bavaria. Once a granite quarry, the site has been redeveloped as a museum of material history and memory. A massive structure with a closed exterior, like a huge stone monolith crafted of materials obtained in loco, the intervention represents a narration of itself. Within its shell, its form hews to a rationale of quarry levels and opens through a glass wall onto a pool of water. Inside the building, which features food service as well as exhibition facilities, the natural stone is engulfed within its spaces. Granite is used both as a material for accommodating other relics and as an exhibit in itself. Memory and context join in a new alliance that sees the site as a work of art upon which to operate. This desert landscape is set against the background of the thickly wooded Bayerischer Wald park.

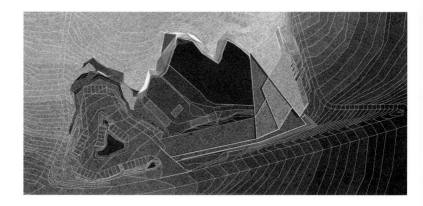

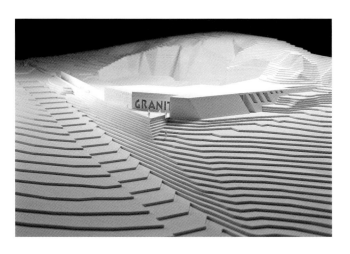

Álvaro Siza Vieira

Museum for Iberê Camargo Foundation

2008
Porto Alegre, Brazil

Delimited by the coast road and a cliff rising to a height of 24 metres, the museum was developed to provide exhibition facilities for works by the artist Iberê Camargo. In also contains a bar, a small auditorium, a bookshop, and areas with workshops for artists. It is a sculpted volume, an undulating wall whence emerges a ramp extending upward from the structure to connect the various levels while creating a strong plastic tension. This undulating wall provides access to the exhibition halls, which are laid out on three levels. The museum spaces are differentiated to ensure flexibility of use. Openings in the ceiling on the top floor allow natural light to penetrate all the way down into the entrance atrium and enhance the strong experience of space generated by the void that characterizes the entire vertical section. It is a museum that recounts the life and expressive painting of the Brazilian artist, communicating an existential dimension in its interiors.

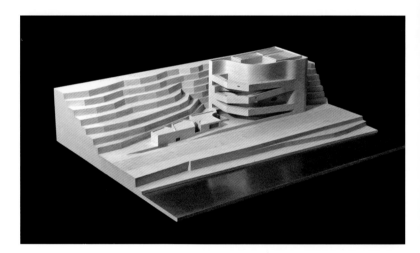

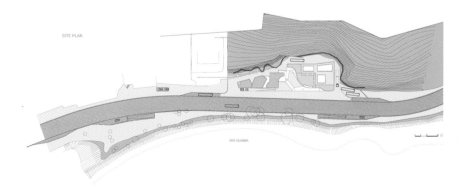

SITE PLAN

RIO GUAIBA

309

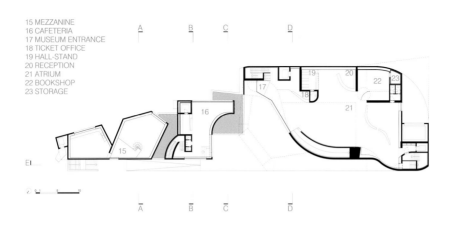

15 MEZZANINE
16 CAFETERIA
17 MUSEUM ENTRANCE
18 TICKET OFFICE
19 HALL-STAND
20 RECEPTION
21 ATRIUM
22 BOOKSHOP
23 STORAGE

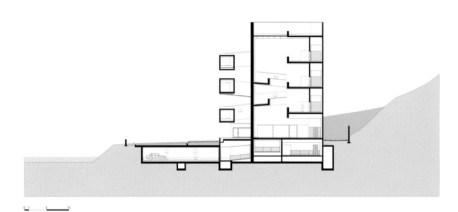

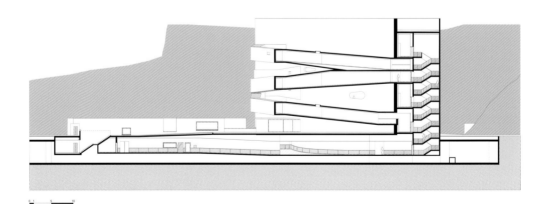

Zaha Hadid Architects   **Landesgardenschau**

1999
Weil am Rhein,
Germany

The building reinterprets the landforms and fluidity of the landscape, from river deltas to canyons, to the movement of mountains and ridges. Inside it explores a natural arrangement of the spaces. It is an experiment that seeks a point of contact among the geometries of natural processes and of those that have always been part and parcel of architecture in an interchange across blurred borders. Instead of marking a precise limit, the project dissolves into the landscape, establishing a new relationship with its surroundings, becoming a traversing architecture. The museum translates into a bridge-building that can be travelled externally as if it were a new territory. The ramp cuts across it, breaking its box-like nature and giving the museum an expanded and elastic conformation, shifting attention from the interior to the external trajectories it generates.

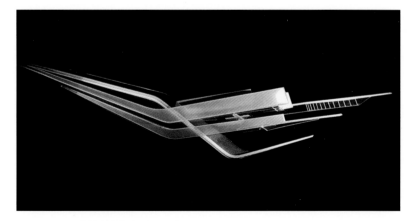

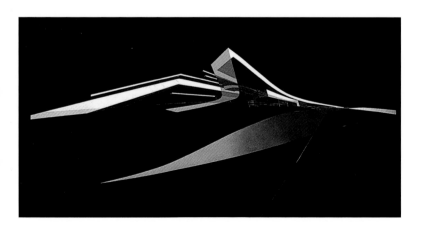

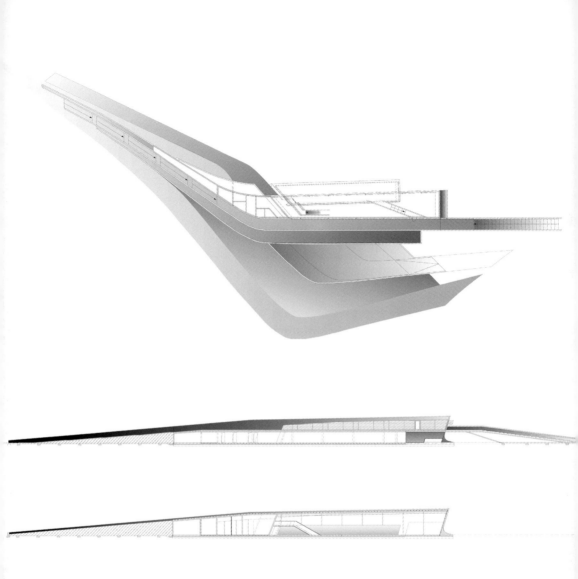

*n!*studio
Ferrini Stella Architetti
Associati

Ecomuseo of Rennes

2006
Rennes, France

The plan for an ecomuseum in Rennes is resolved with a new landscape achieved by a fold in its roof, conceived as a floral mantle. The aim of this solution is to incorporate the architecture into its context to the point of forming a new idea of the land. The new temporary exhibition spaces in the ecomuseum are carved out of an arboreal element, which provides access. Thanks to the use of solar panels, the new museum will provide for its own internal energy needs. The design choices brought into play in this small contextual project include regard for the environment, natural systems, integration into the context and minimum volumetric impact.

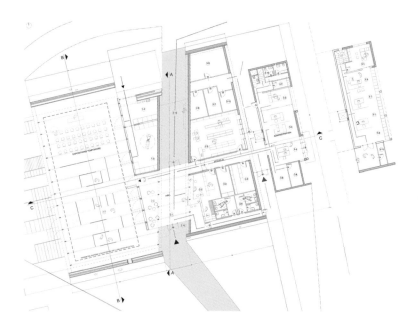

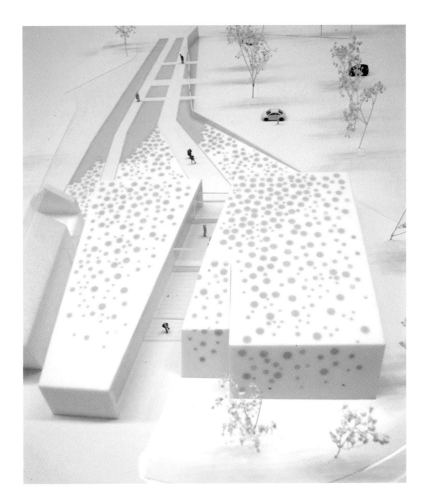

Nanjing Museum of Art & Architecture

2010
Nanjing, China

The museum analyzes the theme of the vantage point in a work of art. With respect to the occidental viewpoint, eastern painting orients itself along a plurality of perspectives, creating parallel views within stratified space, moving on a sort of fluid and loose terrain. Starting from this analysis, the building is developed on several levels that create different superficial arrangements and spaces. An upper gallery detaches itself from the volume on the ground floor to claim its own formal autonomy. The exterior of the aerial body is finished in a translucent membrane. The Nanjing Museum tends to create a dialectical element in its context, generating new vantage points on the wooded landscape. The choice of materials responds to bioclimatic needs for greater energy saving.

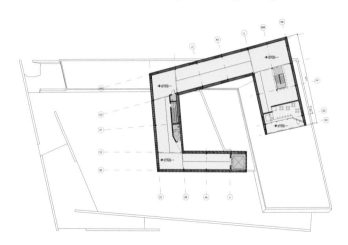

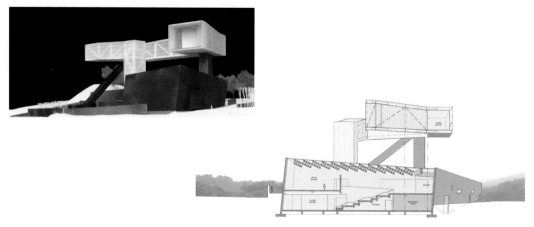

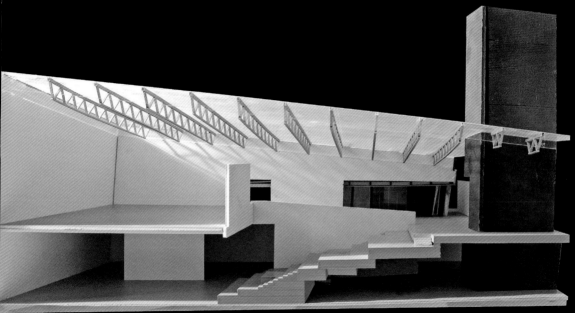

Massimiliano Fuksas   **Musée des Graffiti**

1993
Niaux, France

The entrance to the Cave of Niaux becomes an occasion for investigating the
pathway from light to shadow. Like a zoomorphic figure it evokes archetypical,
primitive forms and transmutes into a temporal gateway leading to different times
and different places. The structure is built using COR-TEN steel. A blade-like unit
provides access to the cave, which is famous for the extraordinary cave paintings
found within. The unit represents a compression of space, which immediately
widens once the visitor has passed the threshold. The building material is almost
alive, oxidizing over time, changing colour in harmony with such a strongly
characterized site and its changing vegetation. The inverse process, whereby one
re-emerges into the light, is accomplished in a landscape of very strong visual
impact, offering a view of the entire city from above.

Design Competition for the Nuovo Museo di Castelmola

2002
Castelmola, Italy

A gently sloping tract on Mount Ziretto generates the layout of the new museum, which insinuates itself into the morphology of its context. The new project does not impose its presence on the city but rather seeks out an intimate and concealed relation, along the lines of the landscape as an inside discovery. The project recovers a number of the recesses and caves found in the areas as an expression of the subterranean memory of the site. It too seeks out an underground dimension in keeping with the identity and memory of Castelmola. The offshoots of the museum become eyes onto the landscape, while the roof is covered in grass, transforming the artificial nature of the architecture into an act of mimesis. This kinetic machine incorporated into the land evokes the archaic form of a hand with five fingers generated by an action of the organism in space.

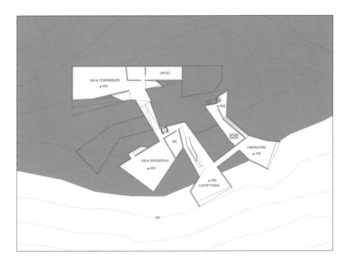

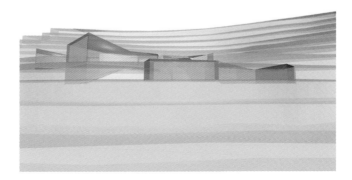

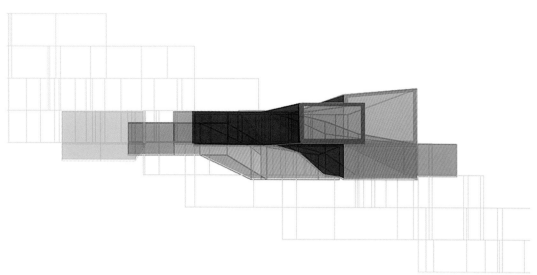

Knut Hamsun Center

2009
Hamarøy, Norway

The centre is a facility dedicated to the writer Knut Hamsun near the village of Hamarøy, where the author lived. The museum features exhibition areas, a library, a reading room, and an auditorium outfitted for cinema. It is an archetypical, vernacular structure that seeks to manifest itself as a tale or narrative. A number of openings in the façade allow natural light to enter diagonally, creating a special effect in the exhibition spaces at certain periods during the year. The external skin is made of dark wooden slats, creating a hermetic volume that is complemented by a rooftop garden covered with grassy tussocks. This diminutive project opens the way to a new interpretation whereby local culture enters into universal culture as a sort of emanation from Hamsun's writings.

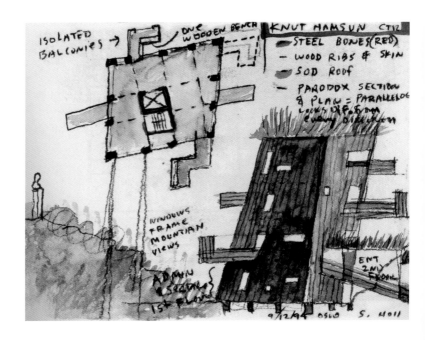

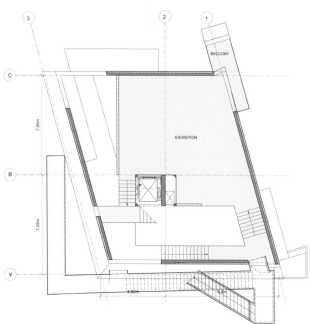

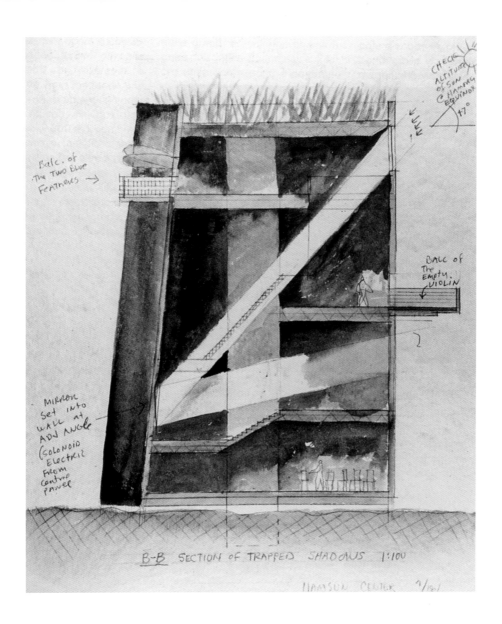

CHECK
ALTITUDE
of SUN
@ HAMSUN
EQUINOX
47°

Balc. of
The TWO BLUE
Feathers →

BALC of
THE
EMPTY
VIOLIN
→

MIRROR
SET INTO
WALL at
ADJ ANGLE
(SOLONOID
ELECTRIC
FROM
CENTRAL
PANEL

B-B SECTION OF TRAPPED SHADOWS 1:100

HAMSUN CENTER 2/101

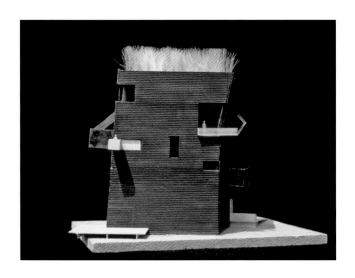

Lab – Pavilion in the Kröller Müller Museum park

2004
Otterlo, Netherlands

Situated in the historical Kröller Müller park, the project amplifies the theme of the garden as an artistic experience, interpreting the museum layout envisioned by Henry van de Velde. An upper level, accessible via wooden ramps, is outfitted with skylights for natural lighting of the exhibition spaces at ground level. The project brings the landscape into dialogue with the viewing rooms. A dual pathway is generated among the sites containing art and the extraordinary park that becomes a museum in its own right. The materials and anchoring technique for the wooden elements communicate an idea of something provisory, like abstract machines for temporary viewing. Museum and landscape reference each other in a new dialogue. The views are multiplied to promote a broader museographic idea.

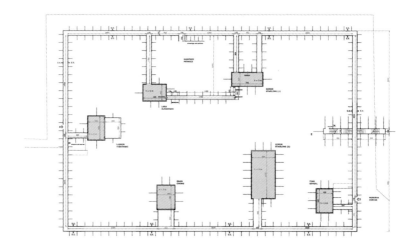

Giovanni Maciocco   **Anglona Paleobotanical Park**

2008
Martis, Italy

In the petrified forest of the environmental system of Anglona, a tract of land covering some 100 square kilometres containing fossils dating back to the Tertiary era, a landscape museum has been created comprising a system of vantage points on the land. They are sunshade-galleries serving as rest and view points. It is the area itself, extraordinarily evocative with the fossil remains that document its natural history, that becomes its own open-air museum.

The wooden structures are shaped like prehistoric organisms and strung out across the soft contours of the landscape. The environment as museum is the new frontier of memory. The museum is no longer a showcase designed to contain something, but a series of special vantage points on the land. The sunshades fulfil a number of purposes: waypoints, totemic elements, land markers, shaded rest areas, and telescopes onto an environment context suspended in time.

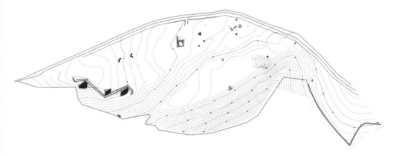

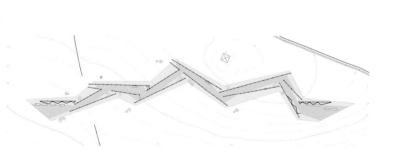

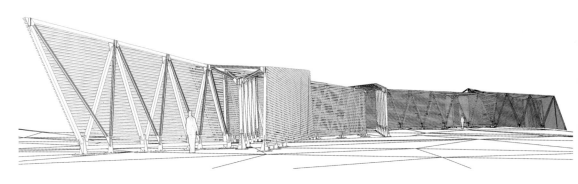

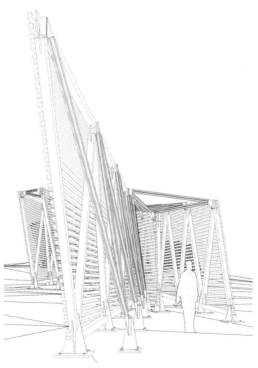

Tezuka Architects   **Matsunoyama Natural Science Museum**

2003
Matsunoyama, Japan

A compact form built of COR-TEN steel snakes across a terraced rice field, integrating into its context. The essential form of this rusty sculpture evokes polyhedrons situated in an area that is covered in snow for six months of the year. The abundant snow makes the experience of the museum even more suggestive. The serpentine form seeks to defy the weight of the snow. From its low profile a tower suddenly rises to a height of 34 metres, asserting its presence in the context by virtue of its stark verticality. In certain special points, broad windows are cut into the surface and frame the landscape. The windows are made of unbreakable plates of glass 8 centimetres thick to resist the great pressure of the snow. The gallery spaces are arranged in sequence and widen to accommodate special functions such as the auditorium and the restaurant area. From the top of the tower, the experience is transformed into a silent dialogue with the mountains.

Ordrupgaard Museum Extension

2005
Copenhagen, Denmark

The museum settles onto the ground creating a new landscape in an alliance between building and park. The exterior conjures the brutal image of unfinished concrete, while the interior proposes spaces that represent a continuation of the topography, reminiscent of dunes and natural recesses. The museum stands as a territorial outpost, watching its context, interacting with it, creating new bonds. It establishes an interaction between the internal exhibitions and the visual relations with the park, making it possible for the observer to integrate the codes of art and those of the environment. Looping folds in the external membrane open lateral surfaces like cuts into a living material. The museum juxtaposes its material and formal exterior simplicity with careful attention to interior design and detail in a dialectic between the natural and the artificial.

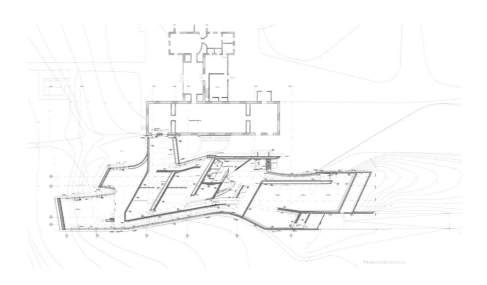

Museum of Contemporary Art

2006
Lima, Peru

The project is driven by a dual motive: to conceive an architecture that disappears into the desert landscape of Lima and to contain a classical geometrical space in the subsurface. The museum unites two models: an expositional model comprising a succession of rectangular spaces in keeping with 19th century thinking, and that of the neutral space of 20th-century museums. However, these two programmes generate interference in the object-field relationship, given the different sizes of the elements that transform into rooms of increasing dimensions. The auxiliary spaces have been organized in the peripheral areas: offices, archives, storerooms, and a bar, a library and an auditorium. A series of patios provide zenith lighting to the museum spaces. They are accessed via two underground passageways, which provide areas for installations. Lacking external elevations, the project is a quest for mystery, a rethinking of its inner motives and a reinterpretation of the theme of the labyrinth.

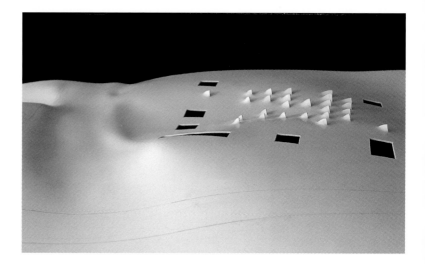

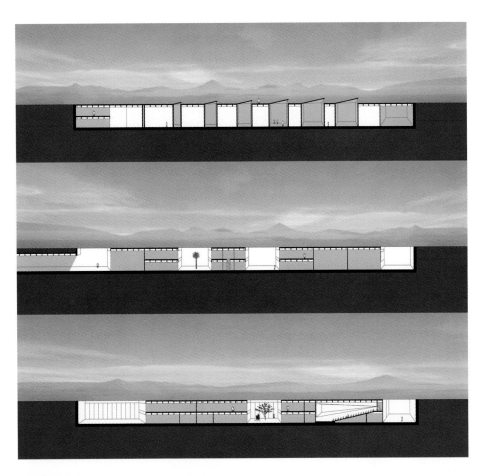

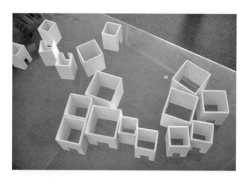
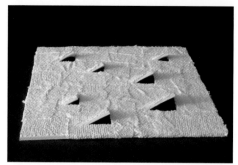
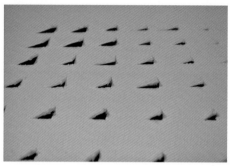
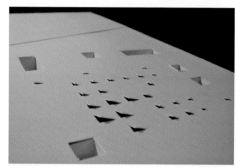
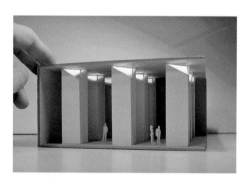
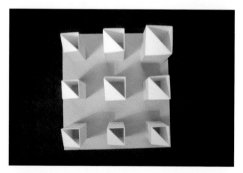

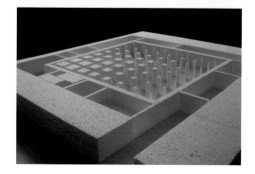

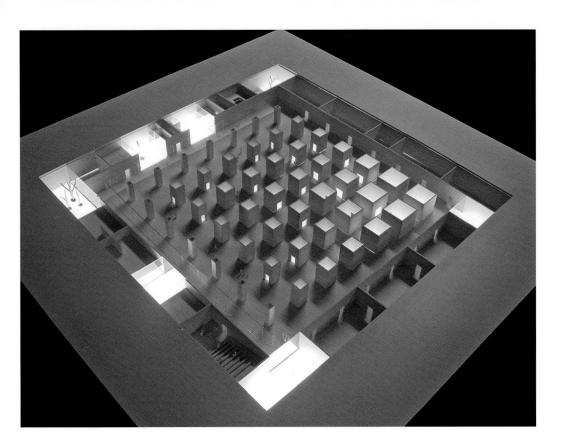

Museum of Cantabria

2003
Santander, Spain

Situated in an area with a strongly characteristic landscape, the museum stands in antithesis to any conventional, mechanical or modernist conception of architectural design. It takes form via the arrangement and correlation of conical bodies evoking the natural aesthetics of the mountains, and appearing as a system generated out of the land. Certain expressionist elements of Le Corbusier's geometry find new applications here. The museum is transformed into a landscaping project. The ground level of the different cones is interconnected by a platform that joins the complex into a whole. It represents an exploration not only of totemic elements but more profoundly of voids and relations among the parts, which generate suggestive interstitial spaces for open-air exhibitions. Here the museum becomes a territory, generating a new landscape setting that is both natural and artificial.

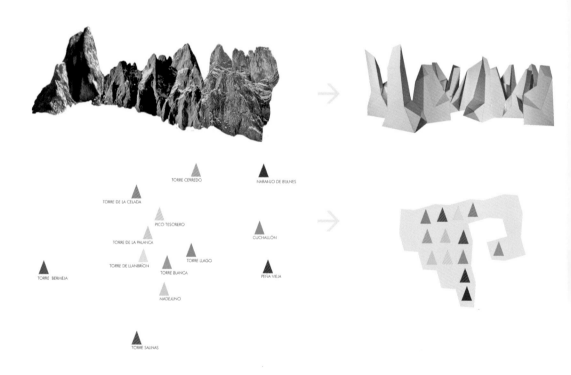

Credits

Tadao Ando Architect & Associates, pp. 44, 45 (b)
Daici Ano, pp. 41, 42, 43 (up)
Luis Asin, pp. 73, 74 (up), 75, 121 (up), 122, 123, 124, 125 (up), 126 (up), 127, 171, 253, 254, 255
Asymptote Architecture, pp. 266 (b), 267 (b)
Atelier Bow Wow, pp. 50, 51, 52, 53
Iwan Baan, 243 (up), 285
Andrea Balestrero, Alessandro Cimmino, 329, 330, 331
Hélène Binet, pp. 232 (br), 235 (br), 245, 312 (br), 313 (up), 315, 340, 341 (b)
Bitter Bredt, pp. 97, 98, 99, 100 (upl), 101 (b), 102, 103, 178 (up), 179, 227, 282, 283
Brückner & Brückner, pp. 156, 304, 309
Gianni Calaresu, pp. 332 (br), 333, 334 (up), 335 (up)
Casanova + Hernandez Architects, pp. 148, 149
Guillermo Vázquez Consuegra, p. 64
Coop Himmelb(l)au, pp. 218, 263 (b), 268, 274, 275
Nikos Daniilidis, p. 133
Paulo David, pp. 84, 85 (b)
Delugan Meissl Associated Architects, pp. 236, 238 (up), 239
Dieguez Fridman Associated Architects, pp. 146, 147
Diller Scofidio + Renfro, pp. 240, 241, 258, 284, 285 (b), 286
Leonardo Finotti, p. 311
Mitsumasa Fujitsuka, pp. 83

Katsuaki Furudate, pp. 320, 321
Cherubino Gambardella, p. 172
Frank O. Gehry & Associates, pp. 216, 217
Brigida Gonzalez, pp. 213 (up), 215, 237 (up), 238 (b)
gruppo A12, p. 328
Gigon/Guyer Architekten, pp. 32, 78, 150
Fernando Guerra, Sérgio Guerra, pp. 85 (up), 86, 87
Zaha Hadid Architects, pp. 232 (bl), 234, 235 (b), 242, 244, 312 (bl), 313 (b), 314, 338, 339 (up)
Roland Halbe, pp. 182 (up), 183 (up), 219, 220, 221, 233, 243 (b), 339 (b), 341 (up)
Fotografia Heinrich Helfenstein Zürich, pp. 33, 34, 35, 151
Herzog & de Meuron, pp. 76 (upr), 77 (b), 158, 160
Steven Holl Architects, pp. 166, 169 (up), 222, 223 (b), 250, 251, 318, 319, 324, 325, 326, 327
Hertha Hurnaus, p. 237 (b)
Dean Kaufman, pp. 22, 23
Katsuhisa Kida, pp. 336, 337
Bruno Klomfar, pp. 184 (cr), 185, 186 (cl), 187
Kengo Kuma & Associates, pp. 40, 43 (b), 82
Jan-Oliver Kunze, pp. 193 (up), 194 (b)
Lin Finn Geipel + Giulia Andi Architects, pp. 192, 194 (up)
Jiakun Liu, pp. 88, 89, 90, 91
Nic LeHoux, p. 287
Daniel Libeskind, pp. 96,

100 (b, upr), 178 (b), 226, 228, 229, 230, 280, 281
Giovanni Maciocco, pp. 68, 69 (b), 128, 131 (b), 332 (br, upr), 334 (b), 335 (b)
Peppe Maisto, p. 173
Mansilla + Tuñón Arquitectos, pp. 26, 27, 28, 29, 72, 74 (b), 92, 93, 125 (b), 126 (b), 170, 252, 346, 347, 348, 349
Duccio Malagamba, pp. 65, 66, 67
Meyer, Scherer & Rockcastle, pp. 188, 189, 190, 191
Michael Maltzan Architecture, pp. 162, 163, 224, 225
Peter Manev, pp. 154, 155 (up), 305 (up), 306 (up), 307 (up)
Antonella Mari, pp. 322, 323
Manuela Martin, pp. 76 (bl, upl), 77 (up)
Mitsuo Matsuoka, pp. 45 (up), 46, 47
Richard Meier, pp. 60, 61
Rafael Moneo, pp. 136, 137, 138, 138
Michael Moran, pp. 62, 63, 271, 272 (up), 273
Andre Mühling, pp. 155 (b), 157, 305 (b), 306 (b)
n!studio – Ferrini Stella Architetti Associati, pp. 48, 49, 140, 141, 142, 143, 144, 145, 316, 317
Neeser, p. 262
Nieto Sobejano Arquitectos, pp. 36, 37, 164, 165, 180, 181, 182 (b), 183 (b), 248, 249
Jean Nouvel, pp. 278, 279
Ortner & Ortner Baukunst, pp. 57 (upl), 59 (up)

Paredes Pedrosa Arquitectos, pp. 30, 31, 120, 121 (b)
Productora, pp. 342, 343, 344, 345
Rudy Ricciotti, pp. 94, 95, 276, 277
Christian Richters, pp. 134, 135 (b), 193 (b), 195, 214, 266 (up), 267 (up)
Andy Ryan, pp. 167, 168, 169 (b)
SANAA Kazuyo Sejima + Ryue Nishizawa, pp. 24, 25, 38, 39
Sam Javanrouh, p. 231
Guenter Schneider, p. 101 (up)
Markus Scherer, Walter Angonese, con Klaus Hellweger, pp. 184 (cl), 186 (cr)
Shigeru Ban Architects, pp. 270, 272 (b)
Alvaro Siza Vieira, pp. 308, 309, 310
Margherita Spiluttini, pp. 159, 161, 269
Rupert Steiner, pp. 56, 57 (b, upr), 58, 59 (b)
Studio Italo Rota & Partners, pp. 174, 175
Bernard Tschumi Architects, pp. 132, 135 (up)
UN Studio, pp. 176, 177, 212, 213 (b), 246, 247
Davide Virdis, 69 (up), 70, 71, 129, 130 (b), 130-131 (up)
Paul Warchol, pp. 222 (upc), 223 (up)
Gaston Wicky, pp. 79, 80, 81
Beat Widmer, pp. 259, 260, 261
Gerald Zugmann, pp. 264, 265